Six Generations Here

Rexford Krueger's snapshot of family on a visit to Iowa became a popular family postcard. Such group portraits recalled and reaffirmed family connections, shared experiences, humorous anecdotes, and family milestones and tragedies. WHi Lot 3994/62

Six Generations Here

A Farm Family Remembers

Marjorie L. McLellan

with an essay by Kathleen Neils Conzen

foreword by Dan Freas

WISCONSIN HISTORICAL SOCIETY PRESS

Published by the Wisconsin Historical Society Press
Publishers since 1855

© 1997 by the State Historical Society of Wisconsin
Second printing 2013

wisconsinhistory.org

Front cover: Four Generations of the Krueger family of rural Watertown, Wisconsin, 1900. The white-bearded patriarch William Krueger, who immigrated from Pomerania in 1851, is seated center, surrounded by members of his extended family. His eldest son, August, and his wife, Mary, hold their twin grandchildren—Edgar (left) and Jennie. William's youngest son, Henry, is standing, while Henry's son, Rexford, sits on the grass in front of his second cousins. Next to Henry stands the twins' mother, Flora, and her sister-in-law, Sarah. William's third wife, Johanna, stands behind his chair, while William's son-in-law, Charles Goetsch (married to August and Henry's sister, Minnie), sits to her right. Missing from this genealogical family portrait is the twins' father, Alex Krueger, who photographed this family group as well as most of the family pictures contained in this book. WHi 2008

Printed in the United States of America
Cover design by Sara DeHaan

17 16 15 14 13   2 3 4 5 6

Library of Congress Cataloging-in-Publication Data
McLellan, Marjorie L.
Six generations here: a farm family remembers/by Marjorie L. McLellan: with an essay by Kathleen Neils Conzen.
Includes bibliographical references.

1. Rural families—Wisconsin—Dodge County—Case studies.
2. Germans—Wisconsin—Dodge County—Case studies. 3. Family farms—Wisconsin—Dodge County—Case studies. 4. Dodge County (Wisconsin)—Rural conditions. I. Conzen, Kathleen Neils. II. Title.
HQ536.15.W6M35 1996   306.85´2´0977582—dc20 95–37595
ISBN 0-87020-283-9 (paperbound).

Alternative Cataloging-in-Publication Data
McLellan, Marjorie L.
Six generations here: a farm family remembers. By Marjorie L. McLellan, with an essay by Kathleen Neils Conzen. Madison, WI: State Historical Society of Wisconsin, copyright 1997.
Illustrated with 164 photos.
Partial Contents: Gathering the family history. —The Kruegers: farm and family.—Photography and autobiography. Meaning in family photographs. Postcards.—Immigrant stories: family and memory.
1. Krueger Family. 2. Rural families—Dodge County, Wisconsin—History. 3. Family farms—Dodge County, Wisconsin—History.
4. German-American families—Dodge County, Wisconsin—History. 5. Family chronicles, German-American—Wisconsin.
6. Pomeranian immigrants—Dodge County, Wisconsin—History.
7. Dairy farms—Dodge County, Wisconsin—History. 8. Photography of families. 9. German-American families—Dodge County, Wisconsin—Pictorial works. 10. Rural families—Dodge County, Wisconsin—Pictorial works. 11. Family farms-Dodge County, Wisconsin—Pictorial works. 12. Dodge County, Wisconsin—Social life and customs—Pictorial works. 13. German-American dairy farmers—Dodge County, Wisconsin—History. I. Conzen, Kathleen Neils. II. State Historical Society of Wisconsin. III. Title. IV. Title: Farm family remembers. V. Title: Here six generations.
301.45131 or 921 or 977.582
Alternative CIP prepared by Sanford Berman, Head Cataloger, at Hennepin County Library, Edina, Minnesota.

First printing supported by the National Endowment for the Humanities.

CONTENTS

FOREWORD

In 2012, Old World Wisconsin unveiled a new interactive and immersive experience designed to give guests a firsthand encounter with farm life in 1880s Wisconsin. Simply called "Life on the Farm," the new program is staged on a reconstructed German American family farmstead that includes the relocated and restored Washington County home of Friedrich and Sophia Koepsell. To participate in the program, Old World Wisconsin guests select from six possible personas, each one representing a member of the extended Krueger family, the subject of *Six Generations Here*. Guests can then pick from a distinct list of chores to perform based on the age and gender of the family member in 1880. By becoming, if only for a short time, eighteen-year-old Hannah Goetsch or thirty-five-year-old August Krueger and undertaking the tasks they might have performed on their late nineteenth-century farm—donning wooden barn shoes and checking for eggs, splitting wood into stove kindling and using a hand-cranked mill to crack corn for chicken feed—visitors from the twenty-first century can connect to a person, time, and place from our past in a unique and memorable way. "Life on the Farm" inspires a sense of curiosity about farm life in nineteenth-century Wisconsin and creates a desire to learn more.

Old World Wisconsin's reconstruction of the Koepsell farmhouse, seen here, was guided by the photographs and records of the Krueger family, who shared a similar Pomeranian heritage. Photo by Old World Wisconsin.

This book, *Six Generations Here,* was an invaluable resource for developing the program and now serves as a companion to the Old World Wisconsin experience, providing an opportunity for guests to dive deeper and extend learning beyond their initial hands-on activities.

When "Life on the Farm" program designers were working to create portals through which Old World Wisconsin guests could access the past, they naturally turned to the Krueger family, who shared a similar Pomeranian heritage and agricultural pursuits with the Koepsells. The same photographs taken by Alex Krueger and his cousins that appear in *Six Generations Here* helped guide the initial reconstruction of the Koepsell farmhouse and surrounding farmstead landscape in the 1970s. It was then that author Marjorie McLellan, working as an intern on the Old World Wisconsin project in 1976, was first introduced to the Krueger family photos and the stories they represented. McLellan's study of the photographs was augmented by oral histories that placed the images within a fascinating family story. Ultimately, the photographs, family narratives, and the author's extensive research on the Kruegers and their world culminated in this book.

In the following pages, Marjorie McLellan pieces together select examples from Krueger family stories and photographs, now preserved at the Wisconsin Historical Society, filling in any gaps in understanding with her own careful historical research and well-crafted text. She opens the doors to multiple generations of this one family, not because of their notable contributions to American history, but due to the familiarity of their stories to "other families in other places as they struggled to cope with change and to create a shared sense of who they were and where they came from." Kathleen Neils Conzen's chapter complements McLellan's work, providing further context on German immigration and settlement in nineteenth-century Wisconsin.

As you explore the Krueger family photographs in this book, the period clothing, farm landscapes, and activities and modes of transportation may seem foreign. However, you will recognize familiar subjects from your own family albums—mugging for the camera, children playing with toys, family celebrations and rites of passage. Like the "Life on the Farm" program inspired by the Krueger family, *Six Generations Here* allows you not only to explore a family's experiences from our shared past, but to compare how these moments are both similar to and different from your own family memories.

Dan Freas

Director
Old World Wisconsin

Six Generations Here

INTRODUCTION
SIX GENERATIONS HERE

IN 1899, Alexander Krueger, the grandson of Pomeranian immigrants, a young Wisconsin farmer, and "an up and going sort of fellow," took up a new hobby: photography. Alex photographed his family and neighborhood in exuberant detail and, together with his sister Sarah Krueger and their cousins, initiated a family tradition of photography that is still carried on today.

I first came upon the Krueger photographs in 1976 as an intern at the State Historical Society of Wisconsin's outdoor museum of immigration and rural life, Old World Wisconsin.[1] Because of Alex's penchant for photographing the remnants and survivals of the passing immigrant generation, the photographs were useful to the staff in reconstructing a Pomeranian immigrant farm at the museum. Fresh from a graduate program in American folk culture, I was mystified by split-rail fences and *Fachwerk* or half-timber farmhouses.

When she was ten years old, Jennie Krueger dressed up in the Kruegers' version of traditional ethnic dress: her great-grandmother's skirt and wooden-soled shoes and braided hair bound around her head. The props—a spinning wheel and yarn-winder, the bench and basket made by her great-grandfather William, a candle lantern and a bell—arranged against the back drop of a Fachwerk barn, symbolize the hand skills of the generation then passing from the scene. WHi(K91)400

But most puzzling of all was a series of photographs in which these otherwise fairly ordinary, turn-of-the-century farmers dressed up haphazardly, sometimes comically, in folk or "peasant" garb and posed with old-timey props: a long-stemmed clay pipe, a spinning wheel, a carved stool, a lantern, and so on. Curious about ethnic identity and the immigrant family experience, I sought out and interviewed the photographer's son, Edgar Krueger, who was then seventy-six years old. I learned that the research photographs were merely a sample from a larger collection of almost a thousand early twentieth-century, glass-plate negatives—and moreover that these images were complemented by a storehouse of artifacts and documents accumulated on the family's "century farm" in Dodge County, Wisconsin.

Gathering the Family History

The photographs led me to a larger, extended family history and to new perceptions and interpretations of the ways in which immigrant settlers lived their lives and how their descendants viewed themselves and their past. All who had a glimpse of the Krueger materials were intrigued by these extensive photographic collections of a family that was quick

1

Ed and Martha Wendorf and William Krueger in front of the Wendorf Fachwerk *house; its unusual carved wooden "hex signs" at the eaves and dark painted half-timbers at the end of the building convey something of the style that, on the Krueger farmhouse, was hidden by wood siding.* WHi(K91)349

to adopt new equipment and farming practices and eager to keep up with contemporary consumer tastes; yet also a family that played at dressing up for immigrant "scenes" or tableaux.

As we talked, Edgar's second cousin, Lester Buelke, would sometimes open up sheds filled with worn, wooden farm implements, spinning wheels, vintage automobiles, clocks, toys, tools, firearms, and piles of glass-plate negatives with flaked and peeling emulsion. Lester's father, Willie Buelke, had assembled this rich, idiosyncratic memorial to both old-time implements and a "new" technology that is now passing from living memory.

The more we saw of these amazing resources, the clearer it became that a significant area of family history was lacking; namely, the experiences and perspectives of women. I therefore sought out women of the next generation: Edgar's daughter, Shirley Krueger Oestreich, and his daughter-in-law, Bea Oestreich Krueger. (Shirley and her brother Bob had married cousins, Delbert and Bea Oestreich.) I also talked with relatives beyond the Watertown area to fill in this dimension of the family experience. In a Chicago nursing home, I interviewed Alex's cousin Selma Krueger Abel, who had grown up on a farm near Watertown and vividly recalled childhood visits with their immigrant grandparents. In Iowa, I visited several farms and interviewed a cluster of Krueger cousins, including ninety-six-year-old Lorena Goetsch Evans and the twin Hanneman brothers, who were then in their eighties. These forays elicited additional details about key family figures and experiences, and began to suggest the enduring significance of both religion and extended family connections.

My colleagues and I initially proposed an exhibit exploring (as we said) "the dynamics of ethnicity, continuity of tradition, and identity in a rural German-American community." From the Kruegers and their relatives, we learned about the history of the local Pomeranian-American community and traditions of rural German-American culture. When we were not interviewing Krueger kin or listening to our tape-recorded interviews, we were winnowing through attics, safe-deposit boxes, microfilmed newspapers, and drawers of family papers and artifacts, or visiting more distant kin.

The results of our research established that, while the Kruegers were family photographers and archivists on a grand scale, they were not bound by local traditions or Pomeranian folk practices. To be sure, Edgar Krueger spoke of going "down by there," or about the Watertown *Vieh* market (cattle fair), or of the seasonal "trashing" (threshing) of the grain. But the Kruegers were not inflexible Germanic types, immersed in a conservative ethnic or folk culture. In fact, they were interested in new technology; they did not keep up the old ways in speech, dress, or diet. Instead, as they and their neighbors informed me, they were an "up and coming" family, situated right in the American mainstream for much of their history. They wove the strands of who they were, where they came from, and where they had been into a distinctively American identity.

The more we studied the Krueger photographs and stories, the more we began to pay attention to how the family constructed and used their past in order to articulate a shared identity. We found that photographs and stories, the stuff of family nostalgia, offered a dramatic window on both the

3

history of rural immigrant life and the processes by which a family constructed its identity.[2]

The Kruegers and their kin had interpreted their past flexibly and strategically to meet their needs over the course of a century and a half. The Kruegers had Pomeranian origins, but they did not persist in traditional ways; they were rural, but gradually they established strong urban connections; they saved their old tools, but they were fascinated with the new technology of farming and photography as well as the American industrial know-how glamorized at the World's Columbian Exposition of 1893, which they visited in Chicago. They treasured family heirlooms and the hand-made objects of disappearing crafts; but otherwise the contents of their homes, even at the turn of the century, were so typically American that they could have come straight out of a Sears catalog. Ethnic identity was but one strong

House, farm, and livestock embodied the success immigrants sought in Wisconsin and were the oft repeated subjects of itinerant and family photography. Alex Krueger repeatedly photographed the family farm buildings. The log house (left) was dragged onto the farm from the neighboring property when the family patriarch remarried and sold the farm to his eldest son. The house, woodworking shop, fences, and sheds were torn down after William Krueger's death in 1908. Between 1871 and 1879, Andreas L. Dahl, a Norwegian-American photographer, traveled to nearby towns and rural locales from his cabinetmaker brother's shop in DeForest. His clients—ministers, farmers, and others—could purchase commercial views along with stereographs of their families, homes, and belongings. WHi(K91)61 (left) and WHi(D31)362

strand of their lives, interwoven with popular culture, religion, community involvement, scientific farming practices, and other cultural strands from which the Kruegers constructed both their identity as a family and their way of life.

The Collections

For more than a century, the State Historical Society of Wisconsin has amassed major national collections documenting immigration as well as ethnic, labor, and social history. The Society library and archives preserve local and foreign-language newspapers, records of settlement patterns in the state, personal documents, observations, descriptions, and recollections. These resources are complemented by an emphasis on visual history, expanded by Paul Vanderbilt, late curator of the Iconographic Collections, and his successor George A. Talbot. Commitment to the study of Wisconsin's ethnic heritage and the burgeoning concern for historic buildings coalesced in plans for the outdoor ethnic museum, Old World Wisconsin. The Krueger collection of family papers and photographs promised to enrich both the state's social history collections and the historical research crucial to Old World Wisconsin's mission.

In order to place Alex Krueger's photographs in the context of other pre-World War I, rural midwestern family collections, George Talbot and I traveled to the Minnesota Historical Society, the Norwegian-American Museum in Decorah, Iowa, and the Iowa Historical Society in Iowa City.[3] As we discovered, however, such large, well-documented family collections maintained intact are rare; as a result, there are few useful models for comparison. In the end,

our richest comparative resources were the collections of glass-plate negatives held by the Krueger cousins. Alex's family photographs were characterized by stiff, self-conscious formality as well as by the sheer quantity of images produced.

On the other hand, their cousin Willie Buelke had, in the early 1900s, worked for some months in a photographer's studio; so his photos instead documented the familiar, informal interactions of children and family as well as the local Dodge County scene, including factories and shops.

Rexford Krueger, a younger and urban cousin, was influenced more by amateur camera publications and the popularity of artists like photographer Edward Steichen. His youthful photographs are playful and full of play-acting; as he matured, Rexford's photographs of family life conveyed more intimacy than those of his cousins. However, each photographer, collaborating with his or her subjects, constructed an idealized representation of self and family, of values and associations, to share and pass on to others.

In the course of our research, Alex's glass-plate negatives were brought in, cleaned, printed, and jacketed. As they were being readied for printing, Edgar Krueger delighted us by presenting all of them to the State Historical Society. More than a thousand Buelke and Rexford Krueger negatives were later contributed to the Society by the photographers' children. As a result of our research and the Kruegers' generosity, the Society amassed eighty-seven hours of abstracted oral history interviews, more than 2,000 glass-plate negatives, many additional photographs, and three microfilm reels of family documents.

Alex Krueger took many formal portraits, often with symbolic objects. In this photograph, dated about 1910, his wife, Flora, sits on a stool handed down in her own family. Eighty years later her grandson Bob Krueger would take pains to strip, refinish, and display the stool with other family memorabilia. WHi(K91)417

Memory and Family Identity

This collection of photographic essays is not an exercise in nostalgia or a eulogy for a rural, ethnic family past. Rather, it is a study of how generations have, over time, merged what has been transmitted from the past with both their own life experience and the popular developments of their day into a personal and collective identity. Following that first interview in 1976, Edgar Krueger and I gradually became close friends, and I came to realize that Edgar valued truth and accuracy. He did not want us to create a history of rural life without the dirt on it. The struggles of the Krueger family as they adapted to new conditions and sought to better their circumstances over several generations was accompanied by conflicts that emerged in church schisms, community disputes, and family tensions. And much of any history of farm family life is a story of mundane economic decisions, repetitive chores, and small compromises to avoid conflicts that might threaten the family enterprise. Farm life involves monotonous, arduous, sometimes brutally hard and dangerous work. The physical costs of rapid change and technological innovations are still recorded in local newspaper accounts of accidents and in the mortality figures relating to farm work.

Immigration, rough living conditions, and the pursuit of material goals has a subtler impact. Even the comforting gloss of family history with its

During spring planting in 1932, Alex and Flora Krueger contrast their McCormick Deering 10-20 tractor with the old standby, a team of horses. Fifteen years later, Flora poses with her granddaughter Shirley with a still newer Farmall. Although Shirley drove the tractor, she said that women were far more likely to do the "dirty fieldwork," following behind the farm machinery on foot. WHi(K91)668 (top) and WHi(X3)38123

emphasis on patrilineal descent—a source of shared enthusiasm for many family members—exacerbates the isolation experienced by farm wives "from outside" who marry into the family and its complex social and kinship networks. Family myths that imbue the home place—the land, buildings, and artifacts—with emotional significance intensify conflicting economic interests and make it difficult to pass the farm onto the next generation in a timely fashion. Indeed, for the Kruegers, this led to their decision to give up farming.

In the Krueger family, the ethos of the "up and coming family" eventually broke down. The compelling family myths of immigration and success, which had originally encouraged experimentation and change, later discouraged mobility, limited economic opportunities, and heightened tensions. As a result, Edgar's children and grandchildren in effect re-scripted the family story to focus on their rural past and their German-American ethnic identity rather than on the dramatic breaks with the past represented by immigration and modernization.

The Kruegers of Dodge County, Wisconsin, are, in their history and experience, both exceptional and typical. They are exceptional because one line of the family remained on the farm, keeping together a collection of photographs, records, and belongings

Alex and his cousins recorded the mundane activities of daily life. Compare Alex's photograph of his mother feeding the chickens with Willie Buelke's feeding the pigs. Buelke's style at first appears more spontaneous; yet it is likely he interrupted his cousin and asked him to pose informally, facing away from the camera, as if in mid-step. The crisp white apron and shirt, the overalls covering a vest and tie, suggest that this was a Sunday chore occurring when family and kin gathered to socialize and take pictures. WHi(B9)292 (top) and WHi(K91)208

When he organized scenes of his father and brothers cutting wood, camping, and hunting, Rexford Krueger (standing center with the cross-saw) turned his photography into a theatrical event. WHi Lot 3994/324

that document their past in rich and varied detail. However, they are also typical because their story-telling and visiting, their snapshots and memorabilia reflect the same kinds of activities engaged in by other American families as they adapted to a changing world. Because the Kruegers preserved so much of their complex, multilayered history, their experiences, and their engagement in the everyday processes of building and maintaining a family identity, these developments are more visible for outsiders to study and understand. The University of Wisconsin geographer Yi-Fu Tuan asserts, "The search for the past is itself a modern venture. It is highly conscious—even self-conscious; it can have the effect of uprooting people from their state of unconscious at-homeness."[4]

This book concentrates first of all upon people as they adapted to the modernization of American life and society over six generations. Their lives cannot be understood apart from the historical experiences that provided resources for their family identity and, in turn, influenced their actions and decisions. The Kruegers' remarkable collection of personal accounts, documents, and photographs sustained and memorialized the family and its numerous offshoots. With unusual continuity, the Kruegers recorded and preserved their history, and to an extraordinary degree each generation seemed to find in the stories, papers, and photographs of previous generations the inspiration to continue the practice. Despite the ever-wider dispersal of the expanding kinship networks, members of the Krueger family maintained close ties with one another, inspired, in part, by the memories and artifacts of the past. They have used these connections to shape their identities, to overcome adversity, to adapt to new demands and challenges.

To have kept such ties alive across six generations is quite remarkable; more than that, however, this modest case study suggests the need to recognize and examine the role of continuity—the drive to integrate new developments into an existing framework of identity—as a dynamic force within American families. This is the story of the Krueger family of Dodge County, Wisconsin, but it is also the story of other families in other places as they struggled to cope with change and to create a shared sense of who they were and where they came from.

Acknowledgments

The State Historical Society of Wisconsin project, directed by George A. Talbot and funded by the National Endowment for the Humanities, resulted in both a major traveling exhibit, "Six Generations Here: A Family Remembers" and a videodisk introduction to the family and collections. I am profoundly grateful for the guidance that I received from the many people who uprooted me from the unconscious conventions or expectations about families and tradition that I brought to this study

Alex continued to photograph scenes of ordinary life in the next generation: Edgar Krueger repairs a milking machine while his son Robert holds a puppy. WHi(X3)38109

while suggesting or encouraging new lines of inquiry. First among them is George A. Talbot, my early mentor, who infused every stage of the research with his insights and energy, and made the exhibit a reality. Much of the book that you hold in your hands originated in the exhibition and resonates with Talbot's phrasing as well as his interpretations. Art historian Kenneth L. Ames, curator Emilie Tari, and social historian Daniel Rodgers repeatedly pointed out how mainstream and typically middle-class the Kruegers were as consumers and parents, thus helping me to avoid the pitfall of overstating their ethnicity.[5] Robert Ostergren called our attention to the literature of rural settlement and community formation.[6]

In addition to extensively editing some of my more obscure passages in the exhibit text, Jack Holzhueter contributed his knowledge of rural life, immigration patterns, and Wisconsin history in general. The interviews and abstracts were produced with crucial guidance from oral historian Dale Treleven. We were fortunate in the deciphering skills of Garbriele Strauch who translated the family letters from Pomerania as well as German-language newspaper articles, advertising, and interviews. Throughout the research and exhibit, Kathleen Neils Conzen, professor of history at the University of Chicago, recognized how the mundane details of the Kruegers' lives fit together into a more general account of Germanic immigration and rural, midwestern family experience.[7] Her essay, "Their Stake in the Land," sets the stage for the Krueger family and their history. Steve Kratky commented on early drafts of several chapters. Myrna Williamson undertook the challenging task of copy editing a final draft. Designer Judith Patenaude reminded us that there is elegance in simplicity. Paul Hass, senior editor at the State Historical Society of Wisconsin, kept my audience ever before me and brought me down to earth. I am profoundly indebted to Christine Schelshorn, former archivist at the State Historical Society of Wisconsin, whose incisive reading, skillful photograph editing, good humor, hard work, and persistence have made possible the publication of this book and public access to the collections.

For twenty years, my dear friends William Stonebarger and Jane Denny have given my family and me a place in Madison to call home. My father-in-law, Maurice Greenberg, allowed us to turn his beautiful Frank Lloyd Wright home near Dousman into a base of operations and graciously entertained curators, photographers, and television crews over the course of the project. My parents, David S. and Ann Handforth McLellan, my brother, Eric, and my sisters, Michele and Hilary, gave me unflagging encouragement and crucial assistance. They say, "in sickness and in health," but my husband Gary Greenberg also shared with me the excitement, the work, the frustrations, and the friendships from the beginning to the end.

Most of all, I thank the Krueger, Buelke, Goetsch, Evans, Abel, and Hanneman families, who welcomed me into their homes and enriched my life.

To all these, and more, I owe the finer points of this book; and whatever flaws it may contain are of my own making.

M.L.M.

Middletown, Ohio
March, 1997

The Kruegers

Farm and Family

MIDWAY between Milwaukee and Madison, Wisconsin, a rural highway leads north from Interstate 94 through a few miles of farmland before reaching the shopping hub on the outskirts of Watertown. A city of 16,000 on the southern border of Dodge County, Watertown is dominated by a Catholic church on a hill to the east and the Octagon House, a museum of Victorian life perched above a residential neighborhood on a hill to the west. The two are connected by several blocks of shops and businesses along the Rock River, which once provided waterpower for the town's mills and factories. The Krueger farm lies three miles east, beyond the Watertown cemetery, a regional hospital, and a new golf course, in the rural township of Emmet. The rolling fields and pastures, broken by tree lines and punctuated by glacial potholes and ridges, lie in the heart of Wisconsin dairy country. The rich black earth was brought under the plow in the mid-nineteenth century by Yankees as well as by German, Irish, and Welsh immigrants.

Photographs like this, in which generations work together in the fields or pass on skills, cloaked in sentimentality the crucial economic relations represented by annual production, mortgages, and inheritance. This carefully composed picture was captioned "Husking corn out of a stack. August, Edgar, Mrs. Alex, Sarah, Jennie and Mrs. August Krueger, circa 1903." WHi(K91)352

Immigrant Farmers

In 1851, Alexander Krueger's Germanic grandparents Wilhelm Krüger—he later Anglicized the name to William Krueger—Wilhelmina (or Minnie) Krueger, and their three children left their home in Pomerania to join William's uncle in Wisconsin. Pomerania, bordering the Baltic Sea, was a province of east Prussia. (Since World War II, it has been divided between Germany and Poland.) During and following the Napoleonic wars of the early nineteenth century the world of lord, peasant, and village craftsman collapsed in the North German states, which included Prussia and the province of Pomerania. People were thrown off the land, pressed into the army, and forced to work for ever-shrinking returns. Disillusion and upheaval spread everywhere.[1] In 1866, fifteen years after his departure for North America, William Krueger's mother wrote: "Everything takes a turn for the worse for the day-laborers. Many people are leaving and the field has to be cultivated. So many houses are empty and still people continue to leave."

Pushed by conditions in Germany, immigrants like the Kruegers were also pulled toward America by reports from relatives and by promoters of railroads and steamship lines. An uncle had, according to

It is likely that Heinrich and Emilie Krueger, who remained in Pomerania, sent this photograph of themselves to Heinrich's brother, William, in Wisconsin. WHi(X3)37862

family tradition, sent glowing reports of opportunities in Lebanon, a rural township dominated by Pomeranian religious dissenters, conservative "Old Lutherans" who had opposed a union of Protestant churches in Prussia and had settled in southeast Wisconsin in the 1840s.[2] These immigrants, largely peasants, initiated a chain migration motivated by the economic opportunities that they described in their letters home.

But when they arrived in Wisconsin, the Kruegers were dismayed to find their kinsman living on an isolated farm, in primitive conditions. William Krueger worked on a railroad under construction near Fond du Lac while his wife and children shared the uncle's cramped log house. After two years, they had saved sufficient capital to purchase eighty acres of wooded land on nearby "Zucker Insel," or Sugar Island, a maple-covered ridge northeast of Watertown. It took the Krueger family, laboring together, seven years to clear half of their eighty acres. Both wife and husband contributed to the family economy. Minnie and the children gardened, grew grain, and tended livestock; William made wagons and implements for sale. By 1860, the federal census taker valued the farm with its forty cleared acres at $1,000. The Kruegers' produce, including wheat, rye, oats, potatoes, hay, wool, and butter, was fairly typical of the area. In addition, they owned two horses, two oxen, three cows, three sheep, a pig, and seventy-five dollars' worth of farm implements.

Henry, the Kruegers' eighth and last child, was born in 1861; two children had died in infancy. The second generation soon fanned out from the family farm in search of economic opportunity, working variously as field hands, domestics, or store clerks. In 1864, nineteen-year-old August Krueger left home and went to work on a Lake Michigan fishing vessel. The teenaged daughters, Emilie and Bertha Albertina Krueger (the oldest child born in Wisconsin, named for her deceased sister), found work on nearby farms.

By 1866, the cash income from William's wagon and implement trade enabled them to sell their marshy holdings and to buy an eighty-acre farm with more cleared land in rural Emmet township, bringing the family closer to the opportunities and

markets of the city of Watertown. In a third move three years later, the Kruegers paid $3,000 for the farm that they owned until the 1980s, along the same road and only a few miles from Watertown.

Minnie Krueger died in 1870, leaving William with six children ranging in age from eight to twenty-five. Their oldest son, August, had returned home from working aboard (and later captaining) a fishing boat on Lake Michigan. August recorded in his diary:

Went to work on the farm for my father in the month of June in 1870 and stade home and workt for my father till the 22 of September and then bought his farm and paid 3200 Dollars for it and comenst farming for myself.

William continued to live on the farm, and remarried twice prior to his death thirty years later.

Over the course of the nineteenth century, America evolved from a world of local and regional markets to one of national manufacturers and mass markets. The Krueger family, canny and adaptable, changed as well. When wheat was the major crop in the 1870s, August Krueger invested in a factory-built mower-reaper to improve grain production, followed by more machines and an increasingly comfortable way of life. The Kruegers had begun to invest in a Red Durham dairy herd by 1880.

August helped to found the Rock Cheese Company in 1887 and adopted the successful formula of dairy, corn, hay, and grain farming that would predominate and prosper in southeastern Wisconsin.

August Krueger married Mary Goetsch on February 17, 1871. Mary, the fourth of Charlotte and William Goetsch's eight children, was born in 1852 and grew up next door to the Kruegers. The Goetsch family was one of the largest Pomeranian families in the area, and Mary's parents were founding members of the Lebanon German Baptist Church. After William remarried and moved into an old log house on the farm, August and his wife took over the larger *Fachwerk* house–a vernacular construction with brick or sometimes mud and twigs filling the spaces between a massive timber framework. They also provided a home for his two younger brothers, Albert and Henry. August Krueger was twenty-seven and Mary was twenty when their first child, Alexander, was born on December 23, 1872. Saraphine("Sarah") was born on July 3, 1875. Alex

15

and Sarah grew up on a farm with two households and three generations.

An "Up and Coming" Family

At the turn of the century, the Kruegers maintained four generations on the farm and optimistically participated in the emergent consumer way of life associated with middle-class, street-car suburbs.[3] Farm prices were high and machinery reduced the physical costs of farming. Alex married Florentina (Flora) Will in the spring of 1898 in the rectory of the First Congregational Church of Watertown. Flora, the daughter of Florentina Wendorf and William Will, was Alex's second cousin on the Goetsch side of the family. Her parents had purchased the adjoining farm from Alex's mother's family; Flora, like Mary Goetsch Krueger, was literally "the girl next door." Alex's parents gave the couple half the livestock as a wedding present. August, with his brother Albert, a carpenter, built them a two-story frame farmhouse next to the *Fachwerk* house which had been sided over since at least the 1880s. After their marriage, Alex and Flora operated the farm on a fifty-fifty share basis with his parents. In 1914, August and

The second generation of Krueger and Goetsch families in America intermarried extensively, binding the Kruegers to one of the largest kinship networks in the Watertown area. William Krueger and his six children posed for a cabinet view in about 1885. A few years later, William and Charlotte Goetsch and their children posed for a similar studio portrait. Mary Krueger and her sister Martha Buelke, farmwives and mothers, sit next to their parents. The Goetsch's granddaughter, Frances, said of this photograph: "... One could write a chapter of experiences and life history on each one of this family and their families. All in all, they were industrious, ambitious, mentally alert and well meaning Christians with no insanity and no criminals in the whole genealogy." WHi(X3)37864 (top) and WHi(X3)38614

Mary sold their interest in the farm to the younger generation in order to retire near their newly married daughter Sarah and her family in Watertown.

The early twentieth century also saw a different kind of development: the merger of scientific research methods with agriculture. Alex Krueger, who had attended the University of Wisconsin agricultural "short course" for two winters before he married, was an enthusiastic advocate of scientific farming. The prosperous years at the beginning of the century were followed by a golden age for American agriculture, from 1910 to 1914. In the words of agricultural historian Willard W. Cochrane, "Farm product prices were high and stable. The terms of trade were strongly in the favor of farmers. The country was settled. The world was at peace. Hard work, thrift, and 'right thinking' had indeed paid off for farmers; the good life was a reality."[4] During these years, the Krueger family projected a powerful image of economic success and participation in the mainstream of American culture.

Through the marriages of August and his five siblings, the Kruegers were linked to other extensive networks of kin that, in the next generation, encompassed fifty-four first cousins and reached from Iowa and California to Alabama and Costa Rica. In the five decades following their migration, the immigrants' children and grandchildren pushed outward from the family farm, drawn by the search for new economic opportunities. Better land, better climate, better jobs, better chances—all seemed to be waiting somewhere else. To own a farm, you had to buy someone out or move someplace else where there was cheap land to be had. If you didn't farm, you might hire out, learn a trade, or, like William's youngest son Henry, choose a profession. For him, the path led to college and to Milwaukee.

Hard Times and Change

When Elna Sommerfield came to work in Watertown, she met Alex and Flora's son, Edgar. She had grown up on a farm near Tomah, Wisconsin. In April, 1929, they married in the First Congregational Church. The new family and the Great Depression arrived together. Edgar and Elna had no choice but to repair and live in the *Fachwerk* house—first ridding it of the rats that had taken up residence while it had been used as a granary. The young couple lived without running water or electricity—even after the farm was connected to the rural electrical grid in 1936.

As in the past, two generations of Kruegers operated the farm together, sharing the income on a fifty-fifty basis. However, in contrast to Mary and then Flora, Elna was an outsider to the family and the neighborhood; she felt excluded, and intergenerational tensions over ownership and control of the farm further strained relations.

Edgar and Elna's child-rearing years differed sharply from his parents'. During the Depression, the life of a farm family proved only tenuously similar to that of middle-class suburbs. Still, even though dairy prices dropped sharply, the Kruegers weathered hard times and sought to improve the productivity and value of their farm. Alex agreed to replace the old timber-framed barn with a modern, mechanically equipped one; Edgar later recalled that people were "so glad they could sell machinery and get work during the hard times." The new barn,

The Kruegers seem to celebrate themselves in the many photographs taken during the years of sustained economic prosperity when four generations lived together on the farm. It is rare to see the family actually at work; far more common are photographs of the family posing around a new piece of equipment, displaying their pride of ownership for the camera. Photographs also marked additions to the livestock; prosperity and family are linked as the twins and their father stand by the barn with the new colt, "Frank" and the mare, "Flora." One generation later, the family rode out the Depression with only three generations on the farm. Elna and one-year-old Shirley stand by the clothesline in 1932. WHi(K91)687 (top left), WHi(K91)514 (top right), and WHi(K91)269

with its gambrel roof and modern milking stalls, was "wider than the old one was long."

Following World War II, the Kruegers renovated the barn and upgraded their milk production for the grade-A or fresh milk market. Two years later, Edgar closed his father's diary: "Pa died Feb. 22nd 1948 on Sunday at 9 o'clock pm in St. Mary's Hospital. 75 years old. Buried Feb 27." A year later, Edgar wrote in his account book, "Have rented farm from Ma beginning Apr. 1, 1949. $1200 a year and also bought personal property for $1000.00." Flora moved to Watertown and later sold the farm to Edgar and Elna on "April 9 - 1952 at 4:00 p.m., price $12,000.00." Edgar and Elna were far older

August and Mary Krueger stand with their daughter, Sarah, in front of the house where they lived until she married in 1914. A generation earlier this was home to William and his family. Occupancy skipped a generation when August and his brother Albert, a professional carpenter, built a new two-story frame farm house for newly-weds Alex and Flora Krueger. However, their son Edgar, and, in turn, his son, Robert, both lived in the house during their early years of married life. Here Edgar and Elna pose with a team of horses and their daughter, Shirley, seated in the miniature farm wagon built by her grandfather. WHi(K91)441 (top) and WHi(K91)683

than the previous generations when they took over the farm, and this change would tax the family's ability to adjust in the future.

Their children, Shirley and Bob, grew up among three generations on the farm. Bob recalled the years of World War II on the farm:

Friday night, it was a regular thing, Grandpa would get the Life magazine and I would go over and lay on the floor and look at the Life.... I was six in 1940 when the war started and I followed the Second World War.

Elna's mother came from Tomah and stayed quite a while each summer: "My grandmother... would help my mother sew and cook and she'd play with us; we always played dominoes with her." As teenagers, Bob and Shirley took turns visiting Aunt Jennie and her husband Ernst Breutzman in Milwaukee. Jennie's middle-class home was full of knick-knacks and so clean "you could test it with a white glove." The couple made frequent visits back to the farm where Jennie's conservative voice in family decision-making sometimes led to friction with her twin brother.

Shirley Krueger and her brother Robert graduated from Watertown High School. Shirley married Delbert Oestreich, a farmer's son; however, they soon left farming and moved into Watertown where

Sarah Krueger was probably the photographer for this reunion held on July 16, 1933, on the family farm. Alex is seated with his granddaughter Shirley on his lap while her aunt Jennie stands behind him. Uncle Henry Krueger, the remaining second-generation Krueger, sits beside him. WHi(K91)710

Shirley worked for the public schools and her husband for a local factory. Bob enrolled in the agricultural short course at the University of Wisconsin during the winter of 1952 and then worked on the farm. In 1960, Bob married Beatrice Oestreich—his brother-in-law Delbert's "cousin on both sides" (i.e., double cousin). Bea supplemented the couple's farm income by working as a secretary in the public school system. Bob Krueger saw his own opportunities shrinking:

Money. The farm just wasn't big enough for two families. It was fine in its day and age but there just wasn't enough for two. And also, I figured, I'm not going to end up like he did and be fifty-some years old before I own a farm. I just can't understand why they had to wait so long.

Interested in modern farming and farm policy, Edgar Krueger served briefly with the county agricultural extension bureau before his election in 1956 to the Dodge County Agricultural Stabilization and Conservation Committee fifteen miles away, in Juneau, the county seat.[5] Although the part-time position brought in additional income, it took Edgar away from the farm for much of a decade. As his son Bob recalled, "Farmwork? That's what kind of got me mad afterwards... I ended up doing the whole cotton picking thing myself." In 1963, while Edgar Krueger worked in Juneau and his son helped their neighbors, the barn caught fire. Bob was making hay next door at the Langholffs:

I happened to glance up and I thought, my gosh, now who would be burning stuff so close to the barn? By the time it took us to jump in the car and drive over here, all you could make out was the beams.... The barn was an inferno.... I must have been in shock or something. I can remember when it was all in flames, that you could

make out every roof board but I didn't remember it caving in. I remember there was a brand-new baler we had never used, that was sitting on the barn floor and Lester Langholff pulled the haybaler out by himself.... Afterwards, it took two of us just to pull it in the shed.

The barn was insured and Edgar replaced it, but the Krueger farm had reached its limits and could not support three generations at one time.

Bob stayed on a few months more, long enough to help his father replace the barn, and then he found a job driving trucks for the local gas company. Bob and Bea continued to live on the farm and eventually purchased a small lot from Edgar by the road where they built their own ranch-style house. Edgar and Elna sold the herd of dairy cows soon after Bob quit farming. In 1987, the Kruegers sold the farm, and many of the tools and belongings that reflected their six generations of arduous work and their struggle to adapt and prosper were auctioned off.

* * *

The following visual essays concern aspects of family life where traditional ways of doing things converged and conflicted with—and often gave way to—the demands first of a new land, then of industrialization and mass culture. Constant change seems a central fact of modern life, yet the Kruegers teach us how families crave tradition even as they make dramatic breaks with the past or embrace novelty. In "Old Times, New Ways" we will look at continuity and change in the patterns of everyday life and of the family life cycle. The focus of "Photography and Autobiography" is photography—a medium where personal and collective identities intermingle, where oral tradition takes visual form, and where the family can transmit a powerful self-representation to future generations. I will go on to look at the relationship of the family on the farm to their ever-widening networks of kin which reach beyond rural Wisconsin to cities, neighboring states, and exotic locales. I will then turn to the transmission of family memory itself, in immigrant stories and other oral traditions which carry, or at least imply, the darker messages of tension, conflict, and the costs of change that are usually outside the frame of family photography. Finally, I will examine the landscapes and the interiors of everyday life, where symbols merge with objective reality in ways that express a multiplicity of family experiences and values.

THEIR STAKE IN THE LAND

BY KATHLEEN NEILS CONZEN

RURAL Wisconsin is immigrant-made. The defining Americana of its picture-postcard countryside—its often achingly beautiful landscape of rolling golden fields, green woodlots, red barns, white houses, blue Harvestores—is in good part the product of immigrant hands. The families who cleared its forests and first put plow to its soil were more apt to bear names like Schultz, Meyer, Johnson, or Olson than Robinson, McLeod, or Boone.[1] The pioneers who met to urge Indian removal, debate railroad subsidies, and vote the first school taxes spoke as readily in German or Norwegian as in nasal New England tones. The German immigration, of which the Kruegers were a part, played a particularly prominent role. By 1900, roughly 38 per cent of the male population employed in agriculture in Wisconsin was of first- or second-generation German stock. One analyst pointed out at the time that the 47 per cent of Wisconsin's farms that were in German hands covered an area larger than the farmlands of the German states of Bavaria and Baden combined.[2]

The overt signs of this immigrant heritage may not always be easy to discern along today's country roads. The sharp-eyed observer driving through Dodge County's Rock River valley may note the occasional half-timbered, brick-noggined Pomeranian farmhouse nestled in the trees, and cognescenti can read the county's German settlement history as clearly in its scatter of rural taverns as in its numerous country churches. But often it is only in the graveyards that the heritage makes explicit claims. "Here rests in God one of the founders of Lebanon," proclaims in German a tombstone inscription in that town's Immanuel Lutheran Cemetery. "Emigrated with his family in the Pomeranian 'Old Lutheran Migration' of 1843 from Stettin, Germany, on five sailing ships, to America, where the immigrants founded Lebanon." The cemetery itself is an assertion of a similar kind: tall monuments and taller evergreens proudly staking their claim to a Wisconsin ridge and sinking eternity-seeking roots deep into the Wisconsin soil.

But even more telling monuments to the durability of that heritage are the names on the rural mailboxes. Almost three-quarters of Dodge County's population today acknowledge German ancestry; the level approaches 100 per cent among the rural farm population of its southern townships like Lebanon. In the state as a whole, just about two-thirds of the rural farm population claims German descent, compared with about 54 per cent of the entire state population. At most 12 per cent of the state's farm

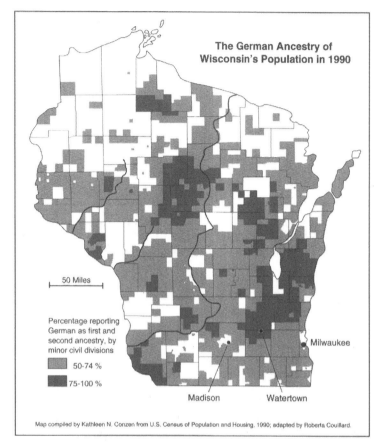

The German Ancestry of
Wisconsin's Population in 1990

50 Miles

Percentage reporting
German as first and
second ancestry, by
minor civil divisions

50-74 %

75-100 %

Milwaukee

Madison   Watertown

Map compiled by Kathleen N. Conzen from U.S. Census of Population and Housing, 1990; adapted by Roberta Couillard.

The Wisconsin countryside may be extreme in the prominence of its immigrant heritage, but it is by no means unique. If we focus on German descent alone, we find that some 40 per cent of the nation's rural farm population presently claims German ancestry. By contrast, only 28 per cent reports "old-stock" descent.[5] Proportions acknowledging German ancestry among today's farm population are particularly strong in the Midwestern and Great Plains states, with only Kansas (39 per cent), Missouri (44 per cent), and Michigan (46 per cent) falling below the 50 per cent mark, and Iowa, Minnesota, Ohio (59 per cent each), and Nebraska (63 per cent) approaching Wisconsin's 65 per cent. In each of the region's twelve states, German proportions of the rural farm population are significantly higher than are their proportions of the statewide population; a higher proportion of the German-ancestry population is to be found on farms than is the case for state populations as a whole.[6]

The Kruegers of Dodge County were shaped by the pluralist patchwork that covers so much of America's rural heartland. The region's culture and history bear the cumulative weight of their choices and those of innumerable families like them—choices about emigration and settlement, about the kinds of farms they made and the kinds of families they raised, about the communities they created, the diversions they sought, the values they treasured, the stories they told. In making themselves American, families like the Kruegers were also making America themselves. Their story, therefore, is not only an immigrant story, but a story about the making of a significant segment of rural America, and a story about how families craft the trajectories that carry them across the generations into the modern world.

population reports any "old-stock" Anglo-American ancestry.[3] The majority of Wisconsin's rural townships today are at least half German, while townships with three-quarters or more of their population claiming German descent cut a dramatic swath up the eastern and back through the central portions of the state. These are the areas most heavily colonized by German immigrants as much as a century and a half ago.[4]

24

But to understand their story—and with it the testimony of the country roads and demographic maps—we also need to understand the broader contextual logics that shaped the choices that such families could make. Those patterns on the map are the result of decisions that brought families like the Kruegers to Wisconsin settlements in disproportionate numbers, and led them to remain in agriculture when others chose to leave. What accounts for the presence of so many immigrants—German immigrants in particular—in nineteenth-century midwestern agriculture? What encouraged them to retain their exceptionally durable commitment to farming? And what difference, in the end, has this rural immigrant heritage made?

We can begin with the factors that brought so many European families to midwestern farms. It is conventional in family memory to interpret migration as an individual decision, undertaken in reasoned response to a particular dilemma like religious or political persecution, economic hardship, or military conscription. Certainly such motivating conditions were rife in nineteenth-century Germany when so many rural families chose to emigrate, and specific motivations like these may indeed explain in rough terms why a particular family made that choice. But they cannot fully account for how that family was able to see emigration as a rational solution to its dilemma, when and with whom it chose to leave, or where it happened to settle. A generation of productive scholarship on both sides of the Atlantic can help us clarify the broader context of the international and internal migrations that swept over the nineteenth-century world, as well as the specific mechanisms that channeled the migration streams.[7]

Traditional European society was never really immobile. There was only so much land, but families kept growing. Beneath the great variety of European tenure systems lay a common logic that linked families—whether peasant owners, tenants, or estate laborers—across the generations to the land that provided their livelihood, and land to the families that ensured the labor force to work it. Disease and early death provided some check that kept land and population in balance, as did customs encouraging celibacy for some and late marriage for most, while war, famine, and plague ensured periodic winnowing. More intensive farming, clearing of nearby marginal lands, handicraft production, seasonal labor migration, and urban relocation were possible responses to rural population growth. But so too was migration to more distant underpopulated areas where, for whatever reason, land lay waiting to be grazed or tilled. Lured by overlords offering liberal terms, German peasants in the twelfth and thirteenth centuries swarmed eastward to colonize Slavic lands, just as sixteenth-century Scots sought fertile farms in Ireland and southward-moving French peasants helped work the soil that Spain had liberated from the Moors. As populations burgeoned with the sustained economic growth of the eighteenth century, the same logic enticed French and Swiss religious dissidents northeast to Brandenburg-Prussia, and German families southeast to the Balkans and Russia.

But by that time, there was also another destination available for those choosing the familiar option of rural migration: the overseas lands opened to European penetration by the same restless questing of European adventurers and traders that helped generate the period's economic boom. English

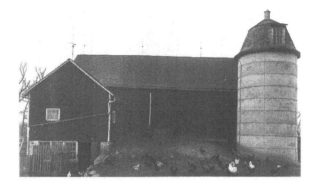

religious dissidents with powerful motives to seek new homes pioneered the new migration to America early in the seventeenth century, but as news of their colonies spread in the mother country, self-perpetuating chains of less ideologically motivated land and labor-seeking families quickly formed. The same process repeated itself in the German Rhineland a century later, as the religious dissidents who responded to William Penn's appeal for settlers for his new American colony drew swarms of German peasants in their wake. Europe's land-hungry farmers soon opened other settlement frontiers in Central and South America, Australia, and New Zealand. But the fertile expanses of North America remained the prime attraction throughout the nineteenth century.

The New World, however, proved no more immune to the inexorable logic of the land than was the Old. As American families began their own westward migration process, the continent's Indian inhabitants quickly found themselves displaced, like others before them, by the expansive needs of family-based sedentary agriculture. There were many rural Americans, of course, who found new kinds of opportunity in the burgeoning urban centers and commercial farming regions of the East, and created new kinds of families, smaller and better educated, that could grow with rather than outgrow the livelihoods that sustained them. But countless families preferred to migrate rather than alter a familiar way of life. Thus, in the decades after the Revolution, New England Yankees trekked north and west to Vermont and New York and then spread out through the Great Lakes region, while Pennsylvanians—British and German-stock alike—flowed down the interior valleys to join southerners pressing inland over the mountains into the great interior basin of the Ohio and Mississippi.

Initially, European newcomers played little role in this westering process, distracted as they were by a generation of warfare provoked by the French Revolution. But by the 1820s and 1830s, Europeans were once more on the move. The kindling fires of industrial revolution and economic modernization encouraged population growth at the same time that they made traditional ways of earning a living less viable, spread the news of opportunities elsewhere, and eased the costs and pains of long-distance travel. Many chose the option of entrepreneurial, industrial, or laboring jobs in the expanding urban sectors of the European economy. But others, like their American counterparts, sought new lands where they could preserve and improve their rural way of living.

The European areas that produced the earliest and highest emigration rates were often those with a previous tradition of colonization or more local migration. The first to leave a given area might well be, as in the past, religious or political dissidents sufficiently motivated to inform themselves of possibilities elsewhere and to risk venturing into the unknown. But once the trail was broken, relatives and acquaintances followed, and emigration overseas became a routine option for anyone dissatisfied with the promise of life at home. Soon chains of migrants linked one European village after another with settlement after settlement in America. Not all, of course, ended up on the land once they arrived in America. Many were retained in eastern cities by desperation or opportunity, while others responded to the promise of developing western towns. Indeed, American cities rapidly attracted purposive migrant streams of their own. Nevertheless, immigrant farmers flooded virtually every frontier that was opened to settlement from the 1830s through the 1880s (although they tended to avoid areas open to slavery before the Civil War), and they filtered back into many established farming areas as well.

Wisconsin, as a frontier newly opened to settle-ment just when German emigration began to mushroom in the late 1830s and early 1840s, attracted a disproportionate share of these immigrant landseekers.[8] It offered just what they needed for the family-based commercial agriculture they contemplated: plentiful government land at low prices and the promise of easy market access via Lake Michigan and the Mississippi. Wisconsin's German pathbreakers were Heinrich von Rohr and his Pomeranian followers, who arrived in Wisconsin in 1839 seeking an asylum where they could practice their traditional Lutheranism free of Prussian royal pressure to unite with the Reformed church. They established the first colonies in Milwaukee and to the north in the Ozaukee County countryside. A second Pomeranian contingent four years later sought richer land further inland along the road linking Milwaukee with the territorial capital at Madison, and found it in what became the Town of Lebanon. It was this colony the Kruegers joined in 1851.

Pomeranians would remain Wisconsin's largest German group, the changing estate economy of this Baltic region continuing to send its poorer sons and daughters across the ocean for the next fifty-odd years. But Germans of every stripe joined them in colonizing Wisconsin's land, ranging from the Catholic Eifelers in Fond du Lac County to the Lippe-Detmolders of Sheboygan and the Bavarians who settled in the forests as far north as Ashland County. Wisconsin's slowly expanding northern frontier ensured its continued attraction to farm-seeking migrants through the last great German emigration wave of the 1880s. Often the sons and daughters of the earliest German settlers pioneered new colonies for the next generation, not

An 1854 panoramic birdseye view lithograph of the City of Milwaukee, on the shores of Lake Michigan. WHi(X3)17087

only in Wisconsin but also farther west. Fond du Lac Eifelers were clearing new land in central Minnesota in the late 1850s, in Oregon in the 1860s, Idaho in the 1870s, Dakota in the 1880s, and Saskatchewan after the turn of the century. The Pomeranians not only pushed northward in Wisconsin, but westward to Iowa, Minnesota, and beyond: in 1866, a wagon train of some seventy-five Dodge County Lutheran families headed for Nebraska's Elkhorn Valley. After the Civil War, railroads and other landholders seeking to reconstruct the South on a free-labor basis attempted to recruit farmers from Wisconsin's German communities; later, when many of the great ranches of Texas and California were broken up into cotton or fruit farms, Wisconsin again was a favorite recruitment site.[9]

Germans found opportunity not only on Wisconsin's farms, but in the towns and cities that served them. By mid-century, when the Kruegers arrived in Wisconsin, Milwaukee was already enjoying its reputation as America's "German Athens." Forty-one per cent of its households were German; ten years later that proportion rose to 52 per cent. Germans were beginning to play a prominent role in the city's business, politics, and cultural life, and were busily constructing a rich array of churches and schools, mutual benefit and social associations, theaters, beer gardens, and saloons, in a completeness and profusion that paralleled the homeland towns that they had left behind. Milwaukee, enthused one new settler to relatives in Germany, "is the only place in which I found that the Americans concern themselves with learning German, and where the German language and German ways are bold enough to take a foothold. You will find inns, beer cellars and billiard and bowling alleys, as well as German beer…. [The German] vote carries a heavy weight at election time. You will find no other place in which so much has been given the Germans."[10] Country towns like Sauk City, Sheboygan, or Watertown where the Kruegers did their marketing, replicated Milwaukee's German vibrancy in miniature.[11] German farm families sent their business and many of their children to Wisconsin's German towns; the towns in turn provided leadership and cultural vitality for the way of life that emerged in the countryside. "When the German immigrant arrives in Wisconsin," a visitor noted in 1883, "he is no stranger in a strange land, for a German welcome resonates everywhere around him, everywhere he hears his beloved mother tongue, and meets everywhere with German habits and customs. No wonder that he quickly feels as happy and contented as if at home."[12]

Those habits and customs help explain why

Germans, once they settled Wisconsin's land, tended to cling to it with more tenacity than most. They brought with them assumptions that all members of the family, women and children included, would help work the land, that growing sons and daughters would contribute their labor in return for parental support in establishing them on their own farms, that parents would retire early and pass the farm on to their children in return for support in their old age.[13] These assumptions helped produce frequently large families, prosperous farms that remained in the family, and children reared in close contact with the culture and stories of their grandparents. They encouraged many German farmers to make the transition from wheat to more labor-intensive dairy farming rather than follow the wheat frontier farther west. And they meant that German-occupied areas gradually increased in size as subsequent generations purchased the farms relinquished by less tenacious neighbors. Thus by 1910, between two-thirds and almost all of the farms in sixteen of Dodge County's twenty-four townships were owned by persons with clearly German names, and in most of the remaining townships the proportion was roughly half.[14]

The clustered settlements created by the German patterns of chain migration played an important role in preserving these customs, and with them the family farming tradition. They eased credit access and cooperative marketing. They offered neighborly aid and assistance in difficult times. They lent the sanctions of church, school, community gossip, and local government to the powers of parental persuasion. They helped ensure that marriage partners would share similar values. And by preserving the German language and inward-looking attitudes they often created cultural blinders that prevented their offspring from perceiving other opportunities opening up off the farm. Germans told themselves

In 1874, the Watertown Concordia Musical Society purchased Concordia (later Tivoli) Island as a location for musical gatherings. Alex Krueger photographed the park in 1900. Joseph Buntman's grocery store in Sheboygan was photographed by the local photographer Hermann C. Benke, about 1898. WHi(K91)124 (left) and WHi(B451)81

View towards Oak Hill Cemetery, east from Watertown's Main Street Bridge. Photographed by Henry F. Bergmann about 1900. WHi(B61)367

that "every Yankee farm is for sale," and to a significant extent they were correct. Yankee farmers came to Wisconsin with many of the same assumptions about family farming as their German counterparts, but they also came with inheritance customs more suited to turning farms into capital than to keeping the family farming, and they tended to rear their children with values and education that gave better access to off-farm opportunity.[15]

Life, of course, never stood still in Wisconsin's farming communities, no matter what their ancestry. German immigrants arrived with no intentions of cultivating permanent backwoods self-sufficiency or replicating Old World farming systems. As modernizing commercial farmers, they sought the prosperity that German circumstances had denied them, choosing their farms with careful attention to both soil and market access. And though they might sometimes be more cautious in taking investment risks and more careful with their land than their Yankee neighbors, they showed little reluctance to switch crops to meet market demands and to adopt new methods and machinery. They participated in the new rituals of mass consumption and entertainment, watched their children become bilingual and their grandchildren often English-speaking monolingual, and experienced the same forces of depression, war, world market integration, and governmental direction that have affected all American farmers.[16]

Some, like the Kruegers, for a variety of individual reasons, may have set out consciously to Americanize themselves. But for most, the very notion of Americanization had little meaning. They defined what was American in their local setting. "We were the founders," their graveyards proclaim. They, their farms, and their local culture changed with time, as things changed for their relatives who remained behind in Germany. It makes little sense today to seek "old-time" ways of doing things as definers of ethnic identity in places like rural Dodge

County. A hundred years ago, young Kruegers already regarded the relics of the immigration period with a mixture of fascinated curiosity and bemusement. But does that then mean that the immigrant heritage of rural Wisconsin and the wider Midwest has little more significance than as symbols on a map or an occasional quaint farmhouse along a rustic road?

Hardly. If the lives of these families changed with the generations, they changed along a trajectory originated in the distinctive choices made by their immigrant ancestors, and the consequences of those choices resonate today. They help account for the pertinaciousness of the midwestern commitment to family farming, and the cultural terms in which it is defended. They influence the kinds of farming that parents are able to undertake and the educational and career choices of their children. They may constrain risk-taking, averting equally fortunes and foreclosure. They certainly shape the terms of local political debate.[17]

And they also, as the Kruegers' stories will make clear, shape the way we view our regional past. Stories, and the artifacts they interpret, are the glue that binds the present to the past, the way we give meaning to the life-paths that we have followed. Mid-America's rural pluralism has often been forgotten, precisely because the stories so many of its families told about themselves were stories of rooting and growth in American soil rather than stories of aggressively maintained ethnic difference. But Americans are now seeking out their ethnic heritages, and the old stories are being reexamined and reshaped to meet new needs. Pre-

cisely because of the relative stability bequeathed to them by their heritage, families like the Kruegers have a kind of access to their family's past, their family's lore, that many of us have lost in our moves and generational separations. Through the Kruegers, we can begin to understand the kind of nineteenth-century immigrant experience that has shaped much of America's rural heartland. We can also explore the way culturally molded choices shape all families, and how families make their histories and ours in the interpretations they shape for those choices.

Shirley and Robert Krueger, the fifth generation here, early 1940s. WHi(K92)16

OLD TIMES, NEW WAYS

BY 1858, William's brother Heinrich had moved to Muggenhal, Pomerania, and was working as a gardener on a large estate. The landowner paid a small salary and provided some necessities—a cottage, a garden, a cow, grain, feed, and wine. From Muggenhal, on June 4, 1868, Heinrich addressed his fears for his precarious old age to his "beloved brother":

We have sufficient means but I can't save any money. As long as I am strong enough, I will not complain but how will it be when I am old? If I should grow old and God keeps me alive you will be better off then, too. Even though I will be able to serve until old age, I will never be able to have a farm like you do. ...Sometimes we feel very much like coming [to Wisconsin] since our situation here is comparable to that of slaves. One can't be one's own master not even for one hour, and what will happen to the children?

For many Europeans, emigration offered political and religious freedom, escape from compulsory military service, and above all, economic opportunity—to work at a steady trade and to gain security in the form of property.

Martha Goetsch Buelke's son took this picture of his mother in her Juneau farmyard with her favorite cow, in about 1900. He then printed the popular pose as a postcard which Martha later sent to her sister, Mary. Her grandson recalled, "she did all her outside work, then sewed buttonholes, patched, and mended." WHi(B91)97

The decision to emigrate was a radical departure that involved breaking ties with family, familiar settings, and a way of life. Yet there was continuity in the move; the first farm that the Kruegers bought was in the midst of a rural Pomeranian enclave in the township of Lebanon. The northern portion of the township had been settled in 1843 by Yankee, English, and Irish immigrants when a group of religious dissenters known as Old Lutherans from Mecklenburg, Pomerania, and elsewhere purchased land there from the federal government.[1] The Old Lutherans drew later waves of immigrants: relatives, former tenant farmers, day laborers, and servants who hungered for land.

Immigrants brought what they had to America—skills, beliefs, and ways of doing things they had learned in their homelands. Once here, they often clustered with others who either shared religious tenets or a region of origin; they created webs of community united by familiar language and custom. They established institutions—churches and schools—with shared language, beliefs, and social networks. While conservative, their culture was by no means static, and they immediately began to adapt what they knew to the demands of their new home. For the Kruegers, many of their customs and traditional ways of making things would disappear and their religious associations would be transformed; but basic attitudes about work, security, religion, and family as the center of the traditional social order would persist for more than a century and evolve into a complex amalgam that still characterizes many American families.

Farm, Family, and Inheritance

In the old country, with luck, a propertied master craftsman or landholding peasant could look forward to old-age security among children who had contracted to support their parents in exchange for the workshop or land. Day laborers like Martin or Heinrich Krüger depended upon the landowner both for their livelihood while they worked and for support after they no longer could work. Sophia, William's mother, described their precarious and embittered old age: "As far as we are concerned, we are being chased around in our old age from one

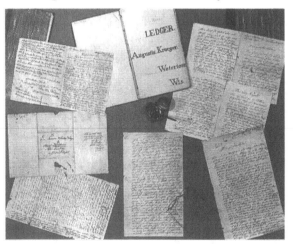

room to another.... We receive 18 bushels of potatoes a year which is very little." She pointedly contrasted their circumstances to an ideal old age:

Although I have two children I have no place to stay with either of you in old age.... I am here by myself with father and both of us are so weak.... Just imagine how I must feel that none of my offspring is close by so that I would be taken care of in my old age.

The Kruegers and other immigrants hoped to free themselves from such dependency by amassing property that they would pass on to their children in exchange for security in their old age.

Near Watertown, buffered by a large area of agrarian German settlement and isolated in the hinterlands by marshes and hilly terrain, they reconstituted many features of life that they had known in Europe.

That area, [a great-grandson recalled] *was mostly all German at one time and they were all proud of their farms and proud of their crops and they were proud of their horses and they were proud of everything they had. And it always had to be through hard work.*

The correspondence between William and his brother Heinrich suggests attitudes and goals that the Pomeranian immigrants brought to Wisconsin. The brothers had apparently parted with ill-will when William emigrated, and Heinrich's letters to William are filled with a mix of recriminations, pleas,

August's daybooks and journals offer details of his daily life and a brief autobiography of his younger years. He studied bookkeeping at the local Watertown business college, worked on Lake Michigan fishing boats, and spent the last two months before returning home to farm "...at all kinds of work, fishing and mending nets and done some carpenter work." August frugally reused old exercise books since the business accounts are headed by names like Abraham Lincoln and James Madison. The books list dates for planting and harvesting, and comparisons betweeen yields of different crops and animals. August also used his bookkeeping experience to set up separate accounts for his various business ventures. WHi(X2)20272

and advice. Although Heinrich wrote sporadically about emigrating, the two brothers never could agree on terms. From Schmelzdorf, in 1856, Heinrich wrote:

...you write that I could work on your farm by day. Most certainly, I would not want to do that. It strikes me as being very strange that I together with my wife should make my living in America as a day laborer and that I should receive the same orders from a farmer, something I can not even accept from a nobleman.

Of course, William had earlier worked for wages on the railroad to raise the capital for a farm; yet his brother rejected employment, and instead asked William to establish him independently on a farm. Heinrich viewed William's proposal through the lens of Pomeranian family and class relationships rather than through the "modern" lens of free labor and individual property rights.

Relations between them remained strained. Heinrich described a scene at their father's funeral: "I met our old mother. She was in tears when she embraced me, and when she said 'my only son,' I was deeply moved." Later, he entreated William:

Dear brother, you write that you would feel sorry if I weren't well off in my old age. I trust this is true, however, you make no suggestion as to how you might want to help me. A man like you, ought to write 'dear brother, if things don't go too well, I will provide for you.' That's what I call a brother.

The Kruegers achieved in America the prosperity and security Heinrich coveted and their letters kindled the imaginations of their European relatives who, in turn, reminded them of their family bonds and obligations.

Although their world views had diverged, the arrangements that William Krueger made to pass on the family farm suggested strong continuities in everyday actions. In 1863, the Kruegers sold their Sugar Island farm for $500 and for $1,200 purchased a farm closer to Watertown, a small city and market center with a population of 5,300 in 1860. At age fifty-two, widowed and remarried, William retired, transferring farm ownership to his eldest son, August. In a strategy carried over from northern Europe, the Kruegers avoided conflict over the control of their farm by transferring ownership when the younger generation married and was eager to have a larger say in how the property was managed. This arrangement reflected two traditional concerns: the provision of security for the elders by the creation of a successful enterprise, and the obligation of close family members to aid each other in the pursuit of that success and security. (Heinrich had elaborated on the same values as he pleaded with his brother for help.)

The terms of the warranty deed between William and August were similar to other agreements in the area at that time.[2] The deed, registered in Dodge County, Wisconsin, on September 26, 1870, conveyed the ownership to August as of January, 1876, for the sum of $3,000. August Krueger did not pay for the farm in cash; instead he and William made a "bond" or contract for the mortgage in which August agreed to provide each of his three sisters with $150, a cow, and a feather bed; provide each of his two brothers $300 and a cow or a horse; pay his father $38 per year; and supply his father with a cow and pasture, a prepared garden, firewood, a "room in the Dwelling house," and the use of a wagon and team once a month. Through the carefully drafted agreement, William ensured himself a comfortable old age spent in the midst of his family and a share to each of his children.

Photographs such as this one from 1901 of the four generations of Krueger men who had owned—or would eventually own—the family farm, were both a symbol and a record of family continuity. WHi(K91)159

Undivided inheritance, with the inheritor buying out the rights of siblings, created "stem family" households consisting of a retired grandparent or grandparents, parents, and children. In German society, young people could not always afford to set up a new household, and late marriage was the norm; so the transition often fell when the parents were already in late middle age or widowed. Family life was unpredictable because, as historian James Sheehan explains, "families were continually disrupted by death, usually of children, but also of one or both parents ... childhood was brief ... extended families were rare."[3] The potential for conflict or abuse accounted for the degree of specific detail used in contracts that would, by passing control of the farm, strip parents of their economic independence. For example, a Wisconsin agreement dated 1890 specifies a yearly payment of $10 to the father and $5 to the mother as well as "maintenance and support" and the use of "1/2 of the dwelling house." In case they were not satisfied with the maintenance

The male line is also important in these photographs of William Krueger and Henry, circa 1870, and William Krueger with his youngest son, Henry, and Henry's first son, Rexford. WHi(K91)16 (left) and WHi(K91)95

provided by their daughter, the parents were entitled to an additional annual payment of $40. Contracts also provided for siblings; other sons received help in buying farms or starting careers and daughters received cash or household goods.

August met all the requirements of his bond. Although William relinquished most of his family responsibilities when he retired, he lived to be eighty-seven, continued his carpentry work, gardened, wove willow baskets, and married twice more prior to his death in 1908. August and his wife Mary Goetsch Krueger took over the larger *Fachwerk* house and provided a home for his two younger brothers, Albert and Henry. In April, 1874, William married his third wife, Johanna Siden, a widow born in Prussia and a member of the Baptist church; their marriage lasted over thirty years. August moved a log house onto the Krueger farm for his father and stepmother to live in, and he later took them back into his own home when they needed more care.

In America, this pattern of transfer persisted for several generations among some families. For the Kruegers, the strategy of transmitting property broke down gradually. August and his wife Mary decided to share the operation of the farm rather than hand over ownership when their son Alex married a second cousin and neighbor, Florentina [Flora] Will Krueger. Alex and Flora, in turn, resisted retiring at all. When their son Edgar finally purchased the farm from his mother in 1957, he was almost sixty years old.

In addition to ties between siblings and generations,

Alex Krueger and Willie Buelke often photographed family groups outside, against a backdrop of fields, fences, or farmscapes. In this typical view, August and Martha Buelke sit beside a cornfield with their three grandchildren. Another variation on the visual representation of kinship was photographed by Dodge County neighbor, Ludwig M. Krubsack. WHi(B91)442 (top) and WHi(K8)22

gender roles demonstrated remarkable continuity in the face of dramatic change. Even as the family adopted new economic strategies and technology, they used these in ways that reinforced roles and expectations. For example, as soon as Alex took up photography, he made pictures that reaffirmed patriarchal ideas about family relations. The male line, or patriline, and particularly the line of inheritance for the farm, was constantly reiterated in portraits of the fathers, sons, grandsons, and great-grandsons. Although there are pictures of mothers with their children, there are no pictures that single out the mother, the daughter, or the granddaughter. Alex, at least, saw a line of men as the center of the family.

Male family members were in fact the final arbiters of farm decisions. Edgar recalled his father and grandfather, in the early 1900s, conferring in the yard between the two houses about work plans. His daughter Shirley observed:

If it was something for the farm it was discussed between my dad and my grandfather.... I don't think it was discussed much between my dad and my mother [i.e. Elna].... She gave her opinion, if I remember correctly, but I doubt if her opinion counted for much.

However, wives who were already connected by interlocking ties of the local neighborhood, kinship, and church membership (as, for example, were Mary Goetsch and Flora Will) were more integrally involved in the multi-generational farm enterprise than outsiders like Edgar's wife, Elna Sommerfield. The tensions between Elna and her mother-in-law Flora suggest that the bonds of womanhood were overwhelmed by other relationships: proximity, kinship, and inheritance.

Husbands and wives shared day-to-day consumer

Alex Krueger took this group portrait of his father and Krueger aunts and uncles in 1902. Captioned "Siblings," August, Emilie, Bertha, Minnie, Albert, and Henry stand in birth order, from left to right. WHi(K91)49

and household decisions. However, the Kruegers' emphasis on the male line obscures the roles and experiences of women in the family. Wilhelmina Krueger and the children shared the laborious field work required to develop a frontier farm. She bore eight children over twenty years, suffered hemorrhaging after her last child was born, and died a few years later. William's third wife, who was in her seventies, gardened, tended chickens, helped at harvest time, and provided for their small household. August's sister Bertha Krueger Goetsch, married and raising eight children in Iowa, was credited with the hard work that maintained the family. In addition, Flora, and other women, carved out an arena of economic independence by keeping separate "egg money," the proceeds from dairy products, dried herbs, rendered lard, and potatoes sold at the

39

Watertown market. Mary Krueger, her daughter Sarah, daughter-in-law Flora, granddaughter Jennie, and granddaughter-in-law Elna all worked in the fields. Elna's daughter, Shirley Krueger Oestreich, described how the pattern held into the 1940s, in spite of new, labor-saving farm equipment:

I think women had to do more work because they not only had to work outside but they had to do all their housework.... I remember my mother and I shocking grain— my grandfather sat on the binder and my dad drove the tractor—and Ma and I shocked the grain. We had a thermos jug at the far end of the field so we could kind of work up to the thermos jug—inspiration or something. That was a lot of dirty, hard work.... I think women did [more work] but they get less credit for it.

Visibly productive work in the context of family life shaped farm women's lives. Although their generation abandoned farming, Shirley and her sister-in-law Bea also contributed to the family economy through their work outside the home.

Everyday Life

In the first decades after immigration, farm families shared a rugged existence. Anson Goetsch recalled hearing that his grandmother sometimes had to sweep a blanket of snow off the children, who slept up under the eaves of a log cabin, before they could

---

This photograph of "Will's old house" shows the house east of the Krueger farm where two generations of Krueger wives grew up. The house was built by William Goetsch, Mary's father, who bought the farm in 1846. Later, their cousins, the Wills, bought the place and Flora grew up there. Edgar Krueger and a neighbor pose on the timber frame of the barn, photographed during its demolition in 1931. When the Fachwerk barn was built it had a thatched roof. Fachwerk buildings remained popular in the area for over a generation. WHi(K91)583 (top) and WHi(K91)659

clamber out of bed. Wilhelmina Krueger was even nostalgic for the lighter work of a servant in Pomerania. The strange conditions and foreign wilderness were the source of other family stories that suggest the naiveté and folk beliefs of the newcomers. In one story, superstitious young August imagined that the devil was after him in the darkness. He prepared to defend himself with a pocket knife, only to be saved by the bell—specifically, by the cowbell worn by the "devil." Change came gradually, and such stories measured the distance that they had come; however, the cultural baggage brought from Pomerania continued to provide resources and strategies like the bond agreement between William and August.

A letter from Heinrich suggests the skills, tools, and customs that immigrants thought to bring to their new environment:

Dear brother, I will ask you to inform me about what I should bring along with me since I would not have to bother with anything that is better there. How about seeds? ...How about hunting? I probably would have to bring along my sporting gun, gun powder, and small shot. I heard there is a lot of game over there and I would not mind hunting since I am a good hunter. How about fruit-trees?... I also have to ask you, dear brother, what the chances would be for a carpenter. I am asking because my brother-in-law is a carpenter and he, too, feels very much like coming to America.... Are houses constructed the same way as they are here in Germany? Please, let me know everything in great detail, how building is done ... is there any collective work done?

In the short-lived pioneering stage, families built log huts and often left their livestock without shelter; however, new houses and barns were generally built within twenty years. Pomeranian immigrant farmsteads typically contained three main buildings: the house; an animal barn to shelter oxen, sheep, poultry, or other livestock; and a barn for threshing and grain storage.[4] Pomeranian settlers often arranged their buildings in an open-ended square, similar to the Krueger farm. They quickly established orchards and fenced in vegetable gardens, planted flowers, and built split-rail and stone fences to separate crops and animals. Along with building a fenced-in garden, planting oats and barley, and buying apple trees for an orchard (all of which reflected Pomeranian customs), August also noted thatching a barn roof in his 1872 account book: "April 26 Drawed and made a straw roof on the Barn." (Many immigrant German roofs were thatched, a practice that survived for several decades in Wisconsin.)

The second generation of buildings often followed Pomeranian cultural models. Around Lebanon, this meant a half-timber construction with a solid frame of eight-inch-thick upright timbers, braced by diagonal and horizontal timbers and pegged together at the joints. Bricks or mud and straw filled the open spaces. The timbers were often painted black to contrast with the white, plastered area. The Pomeranians and other Prussian newcomers called the style of building they brought to Wisconsin *deutscher Verband* (German construction). The timber-framed construction drew upon old North European techniques, but the buildings, plans, and details were not part of an ancient tradition. Instead, when Prussia resettled flat, treeless, war-torn Pomerania in the eighteenth century, the *Baumat* or Office of Building created in 1770 by Frederick the Great encouraged the timber-framed style for its economical use of wood. A combination house-barn on the neighboring Scholz farm was a rarer survival of European building practices. In an accommodation with more Americanized practices, the Scholz family soon moved out of their massive *Fachwerk* structure—built to house family, crops, and farm

Home-killed pork was an important part of the family diet into the early twentieth century. Although the Krueger family stopped making specialty sausages, more conservative families like Shirley Krueger's in-laws, the Oestreichs, kept up the traditions of sausage-making. WHi(K91)110

animals—and into a separate, framed and sided dwelling-house. The farmhouses, with their first-floor rooms surrounding a central *schwarze Küche* (black kitchen), a walk-in open hearth and brick fireplace tapering into a chimney above, had become "Pomeranian traditional" by the 1830s. The same plans worked well in Wisconsin, even though timber was abundant, both because they saved labor and because they accommodated expected patterns of everyday life such as cooking.

The preparation of food is one of the most emotionally charged of everyday customs. The ways of cooking and serving food, its smell and texture—all are infused with memories. Families in the Watertown area have retained the thrifty, German fare including a great many forms of sausage: *Suelz* and headcheese were made from mixed pigskin and trimmings; *Kartoffelwurst,* from pork and potatoes; *Gruetzwuerst,* from pork and buckwheat; *Blutwurst* from pig's blood, cooked meat, tongue, head, ears, and snout. Delbert Oestreich remembers, as a young boy, stirring blood (to prevent its coagulation) saved for sausage, and his aunt described the arduous labor and overpowering smells that attended butchering. However, Shirley believed that her family had abandoned traditional Pomeranian practices by her generation:

One thing my family never did was to make the German dishes.... I think it was kind of unusual because [my husband] Delbert's family ... made all kinds of German dishes–one's called duck's blood soup and they made the blood sausage ... and cherry soup and lots of other things [his] grandma used to make when we lived on the farm. We never made anything like that.

The mainstream food that Shirley associated with her family was in many ways exemplary midwestern fare that had absorbed a great deal of German cooking. Even today, long after most of the older customs have disappeared and the *Fachwerk* structures are falling to ruins, Watertown is known for producing goose livers, and some area stores still sell Pomeranian-style sausages.

Historically, language has been a crucial marker for both ethnic identity and the coherence of immigrant communities. During the Civil War, a generation after its settlement, citizens of the Town of Lebanon published in German a resolution responding to military conscription. Fifty years later, during World War I, anti-German hysteria discouraged use of the language, which had been slipping in popularity for some time anyway. Still, in Lebanon and Emmet there survives a slight German lilt to the accents of the old-timers, and *Plattdeutsch* (low or peasant German) expressions pepper everyday talk. Such fragments are a link to the immigrant past. The dialect, along with the *Fachwerk* building style and Old Lutheranism, helped define the first community. Later, when people began covering the old timber structures with siding and joining new denominations, some began using more English. August, who spoke the local dialect, kept his journal in English and considered "all that German" over in Lebanon to be "old-fashioned." He was eager to acquire English, the language of the country and of commerce; but regrets over losing *Plattdeutsch* surfaced in the following generation. One cousin explained:

You know what our problem was actually? When these old folks would get together ... and visit about things that we would like to know now, they talked German. We were not able to understand it that well and way back they would get together and they would just visit and the

43

conversation would flow generally between them. You just seemed to be on the outside not being able to understand.

Despite the tension involved in keeping some of the old ways while embracing new ways, the Kruegers would weave together pride in both their immigrant heritage and their "American" success.

Church, Kin, and Neighborhood

The farm and the family that worked it were the basic units of the rural community. There were all kinds of work to do—much of it hard, demanding, and unpleasant. Everybody who could, worked. The elderly, women, and children gardened and helped with field work; men and older boys did the routine heavy work. When there was a shortage of hands at harvest time, farm women bore the brunt of dirty handwork in the fields while men drove the teams and tractors. Summer's heat and winter's numbing cold, unruly animals, and unwieldy machinery made farm work arduous and often dangerous. August's nephew, Anson Goetsch recalled the kind of farm accident that could leave families without a "safety net":

My Dad ... was hauling hay in the wintertime on a sleigh. The snow was startin' to melt and ... the wind blew that hayrack over and broke his hip.... He said all that saved him was he kept one hand on that line or the team would have run away with him. He dragged himself over to a farmer's place. He was real tough and gritty.

Photographers captured personal landmarks of the local scene for record and remembrance. The Kruegers attended the Deutscher Baptisten Kirchen (German Baptist Church), a small, cream-colored brick building, seen at the end of the road running through Lebanon. People paid, as well, for group portraits of town boards, clubs, threshing crews, and school groups such as this class picture from 1902. Their importance to their members and families is underscored by their popularity as photographic subjects. WHi(K91)586 (top) and WHi(B91)95

Despite the risks, farming had tremendous satisfactions. Farmers, Edgar claimed, were always optimists:

I couldn't wait to the time for getting the crops in and to see how it grew up. Sometimes, if it's good this year, it's poor the next year. So we were always living in hopes of a better crop the next year.... Farmers always complained. At least they stayed a long time when the farm was in the family. They wouldn't have stayed so long if they didn't like it.

Kinship was a strong connector between the family and wider networks of church, sociability, and economic opportunity. Church, in particular, shaped their family through marriage and provided another center for social life. The first wave of Pomeranian immigrants, the Old Lutherans, left Prussia between 1839 and the early 1840s when the king attempted to combine Calvinists and Lutherans into a united "Evangelical Church." Edgar Krueger described the motivations that brought his maternal and paternal great-grandparents, the Kruegers and Goetsches, to Wisconsin: "The Kruegers left Germany for economic reasons and for [opposition to] militarism and the Goetsches left for religious reasons. There was some persecution for religious reasons at that time in Germany." (In 1843, Heinrich Goetsch, at age sixty-three, emigrated to Wisconsin where his three sons, his daughter, and their families joined him.) Although economic factors soon supplanted religion as a cause of emigration, religion continued as a focus among these German settlers.

Their Pomeranian-American religious heritage persisted despite external pressures to assimilate and internal religious factionalism.[5] Church affiliation and participation united but also frequently divided the initial immigrant community. The first group of Old Lutherans formed a congregation under their pastor in 1843. Over the following seven years, as both personal and doctrinal disputes arose, congregations split and new denominations were established. An early disagreement arose in the Town of Lebanon over affiliation with the Buffalo Synod (the primary destination of the Old Lutheran migration); the pastor and part of his congregation supported the Synod's conservative doctrine and those who refused were left without a pastor. The following year, the second group petitioned for a pastor and established the Immanuel Lutheran church. However, that group split again a few years later over church discipline and a parochial schoolteacher and lay minister formed a separate church with a large congregation.

The imprint on the photographic mount, "Amateur Photo by Miss S. Krueger," was the first clue that Sarah shared in Alex's photographic hobby. This picture of the guests at Mr. and Mrs. Buelke's twenty-sixth wedding anniversary was taken on May 29, 1900. WHi(X3)37813

When this view was taken in 1900, the old Fachwerk *house still stood, just visible behind the turn-of-the-century balloon frame farmhouse which accommodated the three-generational William Will farm family.* WHi(K91)111

In an unusual development, Edward Wilhelm Grimm, a German Baptist missionary among his fellow immigrants in the hinterlands of southeastern Wisconsin, converted sixteen settlers. A church history explains that Wilhelm Grimm "had a great longing in his heart to preach the gospel to the German speaking people and he made long trips on foot to do this." The Baptists, who built a church a mile south of the existing Immanuel Lutheran church, affirmed "the belief that immersion was the only true method of baptism" and condemned drinking, card playing, and dancing.

The initial 1849 converts included Heinrich Goetsch, the patriarch of the extensive family that intermarried with the Kruegers. William Krueger, baptized on October 7, 1854, and later Wilhelmina and many of their children, converted by what they termed Grimm's "hell fire Baptist" preaching, sought adult baptism. While their conversion marked a radical departure from Lutheranism, the Baptist services and meetings were still conducted in German, and membership in the Baptist congregation overlapped with and strengthened local ties of kinship and friendship. The Krueger family, with many of their congregation, broke with the Lebanon Baptists to found a new Baptist church in Watertown in 1882. The local Baptist church had split in part over introducing the English language; despite anti-German sentiment during World War I, German services continued for decades in local Baptist, Methodist, Lutheran, and Evangelical churches.

Although William's "Old Lutheran" family in Europe feared for his salvation, they rejoiced that faith was still a central concern in his life. Sophia had feared that insidious materialism would overtake her son: "What good would it do if we owned the whole world but then death comes and knocks at our mortal home and says 'Man you must die!'" However, an abiding concern for religion, as much as the desire to acquire property and security, shaped William's life.

Church affiliation and participation were part of the German immigrants' traditions and were vital forces uniting the immigrants and the following generations. Although the Kruegers' social life revolved around neighborhood, kin, and the Baptist church, not everyone could be persuaded to join. August, who considered himself a freethinker, engaged in thoughtful discussions with the minister and attended the Baptist church in Lebanon with his parents and wife until one cold day when a congregation member complained that non-members were not permitted at business meetings. Forced to wait outside in the rain, August "never darkened the door again." Henry and his wife, May Maxon Krueger, struck out in yet another new direction by joining a Unitarian church in Milwaukee.

Church membership defined the choice of marriage partners for most of the second generation. The fourth of Charlotte and William Goetsch's ten children, Mary, grew up on the farm next door to the Kruegers and attended the Lebanon Baptist church. (Initially, Charlotte objected to the marriage because August refused baptism.) August's sister Bertha married Mary's brother William E. Goetsch, who opened a Watertown store with two of his brothers. His sister Emilie married their cousin Charles Goetsch, who had worked with August as a fisherman on Lake Michigan. After their marriage they purchased a small farm, and Charles clerked for a Watertown dry-goods store. The marriages embedded the family in an extensive network of kin dominating

47

the local Baptist church. Edgar Krueger explained:

They all had big families; that's how they spread out through the years.... The Goetsches often had the same name, so, to keep them straight, they always mentioned who they belonged to—they mentioned the father's name first then that was his son. I remember my father used to say that there used to be one group of Goetsches they called the thin Goetsches and another group they called the fat Goetsches.

When she died in 1889, Charlotte Goetsch was survived by her husband, five sons, five daughters, forty-four grandchildren, two great-grandchildren, one brother, two sisters-in-law, and unnumbered nieces and nephews.

The numerous Goetsch and Krueger relatives were frequent visitors at the Kruegers'. Mary's young nephew, Anson Goetsch, described the pull of kinship ties:

When families live together there is always a lot of confliction.... The Krueger family was sort of an exception to that. I know the Kruegers went out of their way to be nice and to do things for you. Good common sense. I guess that's why my dad liked them real good. Because Mary Krueger was one of the oldest ones in the family and my dad was the youngest. She could pretty near pass for a mother to him.

Mary and August represented the adhesive force of sociability and reciprocal responsibilities that held growing networks of kin together, providing emotional and economic support as well as access to new opportunities. August may have complained, as his grandson recalled, that "those Goetsches, they visit and talk too much"; still, the extensive network of kin provided flexible strategies and some security to an expanding family confronting modernization. August, cousins remarked, "probably was pretty much the boss of the family." The status of the older son, who remained with the parents on the family farm, may have made him a key figure: "they automatically looked to him for direction."

August and Mary's children, Alex and Sarah Krueger, shifted their affiliation to the Congregational church. Edgar Krueger explained, the Congregationalists and Baptists "weren't far apart in beliefs, but Alex and Flora didn't believe in all the Baptist ways ... because it was all in German." Besides, the Baptist injunctions against card playing, drinking, and dancing were "too conservative." Although the Congregational church had a number of influential Watertown German families in addition to Yankee townspeople, the Kruegers had few social and kinship ties within the church.

While church played a smaller role in the lives of the family, church, family, and neighborhood shaped the Sunday routine into the 1940s:

We seldom missed going to church.... Then we'd come home and my mother usually had baked a special pie, we would have a very small lunch and a great big pie ... usually butterscotch. In the afternoon, we might sit around the house and not do much of anything, like people do on Sunday, or else we might go someplace to visit a relative or go to a park. I know Delbert's family often worked on Sundays but my family hardly ever did. Of course, there was always milking morning and evenings.

The central, social role of the church was restored when Robert and Shirley joined their spouses' Lutheran congregations; coming full circle, Bob found that their "whole social thing [now] revolves around the Lutheran church."

Women were instrumental in the cooperative and social activities that maintained the ties of church, kin, and neighborhood. These networks provided mutual aid, news of successes and failures with farming innovations, and economic opportunities. However, farm women were largely excluded from more overtly economic or public activities. There was a lot of visiting, although some of it—like the child-

ren going to their grandparents' or great-grandparents' houses right on the farm—was scarcely noticed. Other visits were arranged in advance:

Sundays: milk the cows, do your chores, go to church. Then you might go visiting; you might get company.... We were together with the Scholzes more than with anybody else, with the Lettows next door a lot, with the Rabenhorsts ... and Buelkes.

The Kruegers' closest friends were probably the Scholz family, who lived on the neighboring farm; Alex Scholz was something of a clown who trained a bull to pull a cart and later posed for Alex's camera.

A visit to relatives like the Buelkes, twenty miles away in Juneau, entailed a train trip from Watertown and required more planning and preparation. Birthdays and anniversaries were celebrated by neighbors and relatives who also gathered for Saturday evening parties where they could relax from a week of hard work, drink beer, play cards, create amateur dramatic events, and roll back the

Sarah Krueger posed as Santa Claus beside a tree decked out with popcorn strings for her young niece and nephew. She had made the dolls and her brother the farm pieces. WHi(X3)37812

49

rugs to dance to music made by local polka players with violins and a concertina or accordion. By Alex's generation, the Kruegers participated in these parties and Alex himself played the accordion; however, Edgar thought that dance parties were not held on the Krueger farm because of his grandmother's religious beliefs.

An Iowa cousin listed the requisite skills for farming:

In order to farm successfully, you have to be a bit of a veterinarian, a bit of an electrician, a bit of a mechanic. How else would you keep it together? And a businessman and an accountant.

However self-reliant they may have been, farm families were not self-sufficient; they relied on markets for goods and on suppliers for equipment, hybrid seeds, orchard trees, and so forth. Some jobs demanded more people, and farmers turned to collective work as Heinrich's letter suggested. Anson Goetsch explained:

We would run and help them if they needed help and they would help us whenever we needed help. They threshed together, shredded corn together, filled silo together. If we had some butchering to do, they butchered together ... and that's how they got together, and you could call that being sociable, couldn't you?

In earlier days, butchering and barn raising were informal affairs among neighbors. Sixty men might come to a barn raising; the crew set an evergreen wreath, flowers, and a bottle of whiskey at the gable end and when the work was done, the "boss carpenter" would recite German verses before he and his crew were rewarded with a generous home-cooked dinner.

In 1872, with three neighbors, August purchased a steam-powered threshing machine, formed a "threshing company," and hired out to nearby farms. Later, Alex and Edgar belonged to "companies" of neighbors who threshed together and kept accounts of time and earnings. At threshing time, when they were not helping in the fields, women and girls prepared two massive meals each day for the crews. Shirley remembers:

It was kind of like a company and they would go from

The litany of family names from farmwork cooperatives overlapped with the networks of neighborhood and kin. Alex's very complete caption included all the members of this "threshing crew with forks": Herman Bentert, Herman Riebe, Henry Burchardt, Willie Will, Willie Wendorf, Henry Reusak, and Clancy Fairfield. WHi(K91)182

farm to farm ... until they were finished. They would help one another. When I was young [in the 1940s] I didn't do anything but watch ... and do dishes.

Some cooperative efforts were formal, like the nearby Hustisford Farmers' Mutual Insurance Company or the cheese factory begun in 1888. August Krueger served as treasurer of the cheese company for many years and as a director on the board of the insurance company for two decades. He was elected town treasurer, and three generations of Kruegers served on the school and election boards. Membership on town boards was an honor—a responsibility that gave a man a place in the community.

The Kruegers also reached beyond the local scene—in order to profit from wider markets for farm produce; to participate in organizations

The local newspaper reported on activities and accomplishments: "We understand that Wm. Buelke of Juneau took a large size picture of the Dead Creek Cheese Factory Sunday afternoon. On the foreground ... are to be seen Mr. and Mrs. O. Rupprecht and daughters. This makes it a complete, beautiful and very attractive picture." Willie had an established business photographing area schools, businesses, factories, dams, and railroad construction. WHi(B91)247

like the *Watertown Plattdeutscher Verein*, an ethnic society; to purchase new implements and consumer goods; and to follow national politics. (They supported, and attended speeches by, Democratic presidential candidate William Jennings Bryan.) Such broad outside interests both reflected and encouraged the Krueger family's shift toward mainstream America.

51

PHOTOGRAPHY AND AUTOBIOGRAPHY

IN 1873, as a young mother, Mary Krueger sat with her infant son, Alex, for a conventional studio portrait. She wore a beribboned hat and lace collar; he, a home-made dress, decorated with ribbon at the cuffs, collar, and hems. Mother and son exist to this day, their cheeks hand-tinted pink as if to offer some relief from the cold grayness of the tintype image. Formal portraits like this, treasured in a decorative case, marked important moments in the family life cycle: marriage, birth, military service, a new occupation, a significant anniversary. From its beginnings in the 1840s, photography revolutionized the way we record our world and remember ourselves.[1]

Early photographic processes, limited to professionals and wealthy amateurs, produced a single, direct image: daguerreotypes (on metal rectangles), ambrotypes, and tintypes. By the 1880s, local photographers, producing multiple prints from the new gelatin-coated, glass-plate negatives, had become a

In this 1901 photograph, farmwork is represented by the windmill, shed, and garden fence which merge with domesticity, leisure, and the flower garden. This distinguished farm families from their urban counterparts who commuted away from home to work—often by streetcar. Sarah Krueger's casual appearance—at play with "Sailor" and "Pup," yet dressed for church or another social occasion—was an unusual photograph for Alex Krueger. WHi(K91)170

common resource for both the urban family and the farmer in the hinterlands. Photography studios gradually took over from the local or "folk" painters who had supplemented sign painting with occasional portraits and farm views. As a result, the new medium raised new expectations for the content and composition of images that carried over from painting. In the 1870s and 1880s, family photographs were still largely limited to stiffly posed studio portraits—the "stiffness" being a factor of the time required to expose the plate. Young adults traded small format photographic "cartes-de-visite" and filled specially designed albums with these miniature portraits. Soon new and larger "cabinet cards," mounted on a decorative cardboard backing, represented family ties and life-cycle events and were intended for display. William Krueger's brother, Heinrich, sent his thanks for a family studio portrait in 1881: "The pictures arrived.... I shed tears of joy. You could not have given me a better present except for our dear Savior. We could easily recognize everyone."

At first, Anson Goetsch commented:

[Farmers] didn't have a lot of money and [studio] photography was kind of expensive, so if they took a wedding picture and then a picture about the first child or so, the rest of them didn't get their picture taken much.

The studios provided both serious and playful backdrops, but the subjects' few personal props, usually their best clothes, restricted the possibilities for self-expression. This gradually changed as village photographers loaded their cameras and darkroom equipment into carefully sealed wagons and took to the rural roads, bringing photography to their customers' doorsteps. In the 1880s, the Krueger family posed for an itinerant photographer: first in the field beneath their farm for a panoramic view; then standing around the porch for a close-up of the big half-timbered house. In the 1870s and 1880s, itinerant photographers made a business of traveling to villages and farms, photographing people at home or at work. At home, in contrast to the studio, customers could

In the Krubsack family portrait on the left, the photographer planned to trim the print and hide the edges of the homemade backdrop. In order to share portraits among their wide circle of relatives, Alex and Sarah made copy negatives of unique early images such as this 1873 tintype of Mary and baby Alex. WHi(K8)35 (left) and WHi(K91)13

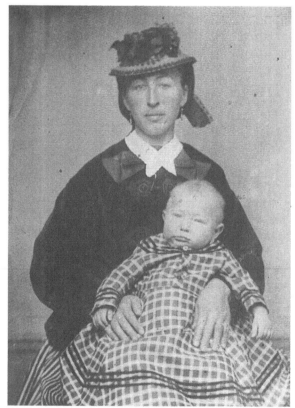

personalize their images by incorporating their belongings into the portrait. Families posed on the lawn in front of their houses with their prized possessions—from china to sewing machines, from porcelain dolls to livestock. These photographs evince both pride of place and personal success. (Anson Goetsch recalled that an itinerant photographer successfully courted a local girl by pretending to ownership of the substantial farm depicted in one of his photographs!)

In the last decades of the century, technological improvements made glass-plate negatives cheap and easy enough to use to make photography a popular hobby or avocation. At home, photography generated highly personalized representations of individuals and groups; yet the possibilities were channeled and constrained by both culture and technology. Alex, the amateur photographer working hidden under a black cloth behind a camera large enough to hold 4x5 inch glass-plate negatives, was constrained by the technology. His camera, mounted on a spindly wooden tripod, required arrangement and adjustment to frame the desired view or perspective. Photographers learned the conventions of subject, composition, and pose by turning to paintings, popular prints, studio photographs, stereographic views, advertisements for photographic supplies, handbooks and guides, and photography clubs.

Photographers and their subjects saw their picture-making in the context of popular imagery and, in Rexford Krueger's case, in terms of art photography. Although home photography was new at the turn of the century, the images and poses fit clearly prescribed genres; for example cute children, pride in possessions, the local scene, portraiture, family groups, work groups, social gatherings, travel, and visual jokes. Popular prints and magazine illustrations as well as the conventions of itinerant and studio portrait photography influenced the amateur's framing, poses, props, and message.

The content of photographs likewise expressed a blend of past and present, tradition and innovation. Early amateur photography—such as the patrilineal "four generation" Krueger photographs and the awkward family portrait of the Krubsacks in nearby Lebanon—imitated the studio photographs. However, other mass-produced visual media such as the increasingly popular color lithographs, magazine advertisements, stereographs, and all manner of picture postcards expanded the repertoire for family photography to include sentimental scenes, disasters, scenic views, cultural events, and a variety of visual jokes. By the turn of the century, a flood of snapshots detailing events, people, and places replaced the occasional portrait or view of a house or farm taken by a professional photographer.

The Kruegers, with Willie Buelke and Alex Krueger in the lead, took to photography in the late 1890s, making landscape views and "artistic" compositions as well as ordinary snapshots. To some extent, photography took over from letters, diaries, and memory books as a record and elaboration of social events, interior decoration, party guests, and newly acquired possessions. The Kruegers used photographs to tell each other what was new, how well they were doing, and where they had been, both literally and figuratively. Their energetic approach to picture-making generated thousands of images which, dispersed through networks of kin, constitute a fully realized, self-created portrait of a family.

"Wm and Johanna Krueger in the front room of their log house. Flash light picture taken in the winter of 1901." WHi(K91)173

Reading Pictures

The Krueger photographs document, on one hand, the social and material world of the American middle class in both rural and urban settings. Although few photographs capture a truly unselfconscious slice of "real life," family photographs like these catalog details which can be "read" by social historians, folklorists, and museum curators for data on material goods, everyday life, and vernacular landscapes.[2] On the other hand, the photographer and his subjects imaginatively construct images in a picture-taking event that frequently involves props, poses, and manipulation of the scene. As a result, family photographs do capture a particularly evocative moment of ordinary life—namely, the creative, esthetic, and social activity of taking pictures.

A researcher "reads" a photograph in order to answer specific questions about objects and details shown in the image. These two photographs of the parlor in William and Johanna Krueger's log house are full of clues about the kind of life that they led. These photographs were flash pictures made late in the winter of 1901. One was taken on the fifth of

William Krueger carved the picture frame for his own portrait which can also be seen displayed on the parlor wall in 1901. WHi(X2)20456 (left) and WHi(K91)172

The array of china and silver in this photograph of "Mr. and Mrs. Alex Krueger eating supper" demonstrates the Krueger's interest in the material goods offered by American consumer culture. This scene, the previous photographs of the log house interior, and the photograph of August, Mary, and Sarah in their dining room on page 126 represent an intentional effort to document the family's status at the turn of the century. WHi(K91)87

March at 8:20—likely in the morning with the shade pulled to avoid the glare of sunlight in a flash picture. The other photo was taken in the evening some time later—note that the window is dark—or perhaps on another day.

The two pictures are revealing in part because of the differences. One picture is more "dressed up": Johanna has taken off her apron and put on a "good" dark skirt; William has put on shoes instead of clogs, clean pants, and a watch and chain. The oil cloth and simple plaid covers on the pillows and chair have been replaced. William's spittoon and long-stemmed pipe and the willow splints he used in making baskets have been concealed; the toys and basket he made have been brought in, and rugs have been laid down on the floor. Although Alex simply intended to produce a spruced-up version of the early photograph, much like a rough and a final draft, he inadvertently documented what he and his grandparents did to project an image of who and what they were.

The profusion of Krueger family pictures—the Hanover School where Henry, William's youngest son, was principal; Henry's wedding picture; a portrait of Johanna; a portrait of August, Alex, and Sarah made about 1890; a portrait of William taken about the time of his retirement in 1870, in a frame that he made himself—all these pictures suggest the strong web of ties that bound the family together. However, the pictures have been rearranged to make room in the photograph for a large color lithograph of a milkmaid with a little girl, a cow, and some calves in the kind of marshy landscape often seen in late-nineteenth-century art. The print, Edgar recalled, may have been a present from Henry— "it was the kind of thing he would do"—in

The Kruegers demonstrate their continuing interest in old family photographs when they restage an image from the past. WHi(X3)37831

which case it may represent the urbanite's romantic vision of rural life. This print, the table, and the pillow covers all show the fussy, elaborate taste of the day. But many of the room's other furnishings—the clock and clock shelf, the day bed, the handmade picture frames—are in the style of a period at least three decades earlier. They reflect William Krueger's craft skills and family pride in his work. Alex probably meant to symbolize his grandfather's skills as well by including the baskets and the figures on horseback; William made these toys, variously described by family members as "cowboys" or "Prussian officers." Even the long-stemmed pipe, which also appears in the immigrant dress-up photographs, may have been included out of routine use or with the intent to express a tie to an immigrant identity.

59

Edgar acknowledged that his father staged "artistic pictures," but in this scene his fishing adventures with his sister were most vividly recalled. The reflections on the water, the long fishing poles, the crisp white outfits, and relaxed atmosphere set against planted fields and prosperous farm buildings make up a family idyll in the style of a popular Currier and Ives print. WHi(K91)282

This pair of images reveals the Kruegers' self-conscious effort to construct identity as photographer and subjects look, select, reject, and layer images with symbols. In both images, newspapers and books—likely including a family bible and a hymnal—represent literacy, piety, and use of the German language. The masthead of the *Watertown Weltbürger*, a local Democratic weekly, and *Der Sendbote* [The Messenger], a German-language Baptist paper, are carefully displayed. Hanging on the wall are both a German calendar and a local advertising calendar from Richard Geshke & Co., a Watertown dry-goods store. The propped-up newspapers suggest the extent of intentional preparation in both photographs. The Kruegers pointedly demonstrated the importance of family ties and religion, of literacy and involvement in larger events, and of the continuing significance of their native language, craft skills, and ethnic identity.

These photographs have, in turn, reinforced other memories. Edgar Krueger and his father's cousin Selma Abel touched on the enduring pull of this scene in their vivid descriptions of childhood visits with the old couple. They recalled the sound of the clock ticking away, the smell of apple slices set to dry in the window, and their fear of inadvertently annoying the older generation. Selma described the warm Sunday afternoons following dinner, when she rocked timidly, listening to the clock and imagining the sound of the milkmaid milking in the lithograph on the wall: "tick, tock, squish, squish, tick, tock...."

A single photograph can tell us a great deal, but in large family collections such as the Kruegers' we can watch people grow up, families evolve and change, continuities extend from one generation to the next. The Kruegers know their old pictures well, and

occasionally the family photographer will turn to them for subject matter, repeating favorite themes or poses. The picture made in December, 1900, "Mr. & Mrs. Alex Krueger eating supper—new house," shows Alex holding a cup. On February 5, 1944, in the same room, Jennie Krueger and her parents recreated the pose, with Alex holding a different cup, as if to demonstrate how the room, the styles, and the people had changed. Other topics, like a turn-of-the-century picture of August and Mary harvesting, were equally popular among family members. (This probably was posed as a "history picture" since cradle scythes were, of course, obsolete by that time.) This photograph was in turn a source for a series of pictures taken in 1944 of Alex and Flora posing with the same tools.

Not suprisingly, some photographs elude both family memory and contemporary interpretation. What should we make, for example, of the enigmatic photograph of Ernie Buelke, in a nightshirt

Willie Buelke photographed his brother Ernie and cousin Sarah in an elaborate visual joke. WHi(B9)242

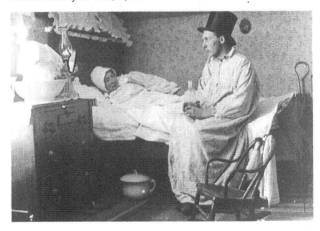

61

At Old World Wisconsin, photographs like these were "read" for the arrangement of fences and farm equipment located on Pomeranian immigrant farmsteads; however, it was the successful achievement of the immigrant generation's goals which the Kruegers sought to document. The photographs which used William's hand-crafted willow baskets as props, sentimentalized the innocence of childhood in a style familiar from commercial lithographs, stereographs, advertisements, and postcards. Economic innovations and agricultural experiments were also a source of pride; here Alex and Edgar call attention to beehives placed in the pear orchard. The caption, "Training While Young," refers as much to the twins as to the twin calves in their miniature yoke, and conveys confidence in the family's success continuing into future generations. WHi(K91)297 (top left), WHi(K91)512 (top right), and WHi(K91)311

pulled over his clothes and shoes, apparently ministering to his cousin Sarah Krueger, huddled under her bedclothes? We see the sloping second-floor ceiling, the flowery wallpaper, the decorative pillow shams, the neatly arranged washstand—the small private amenities enjoyed by a grown daughter living and working with her parents on the family farm. But what can be the significance, if any, of the top hat, the bottle, the umbrella, the prominently displayed chamber pot?

Joining the Mainstream

For Alex and his sister Sarah, photography was a way of being "modern." Their new hobby allowed them to show off their interest in art and technology and to create images that celebrated their family and its heritage, all at the same time. In over a thousand photographs, Alex represented a wide range of themes and subject matter. However, two dominant themes emerge: the family's past, including both the immigrant story and their patrilineal tenure on the farm; and their mainstream, consumer-oriented domesticity in the early twentieth century. Ethnicity and rural family life were strands that particularized the Kruegers' identity without detracting from their sense of being fully American. The result of Alex's impulse towards self-documention is a compelling family autobiography, constructed in visual form.

The Kruegers took pride in the extent to which they participated in the wider American experience. In 1893, Alex, Sarah, and their parents had visited the World's Columbian Exposition in Chicago. During his tenure as an agriculture student at the University of Wisconsin in Madison, Alex learned

Willie Buelke catches his niece and a flock of chickens in a blurred, spontaneous moment along the orchard fence. A generation later, Alex photographed his young grandson, Robert, at play with "Sport." The airplane applique on the child's overalls is the only sign of the world events which loomed over his and Shirley's childhood—the Great Depression and World War II. WHi(B9)299 (top) and WHi(K92)13

Alex placed the twins into this fish-cleaning scene in order to create a cute family portrait resonant with the message of mutual involvement and cooperation across generations. Both children clutch fish, even though Jennie doesn't even have on an apron. WHi(K91)207

about new technology and experimented with a more individualistic, urban lifestyle. He sampled sermons at the Unitarian and Evangelical churches and attended a lecture on China at the Presbyterian church. He wrote home:

This forenoon, I and two other boys looked all over the machine shops where they have the forges and the carpentry work and from there we went to the Capitol and into the museum.... Last night we all met and organized a Literary Society here and we must have a book called Robert's Rules of Order....

"We also," he wrote, "have a darkey in our course. ...He is from South Carolina. A smart fellow." For a young man from rural Watertown, attending the university in the state capital was truly like opening a window on another, wider world.

In the years following Alex and Flora's marriage, the farm family unabashedly basked in their sense of having become a successful and Americanized family.[3] There was little to distinguish Flora and Alex's parlor from a comfortable home in Madison or Milwaukee. Sharing the demanding routine of a dairy farm with the older generation, Sarah, Alex, and Flora Krueger had the freedom to visit relatives in Milwaukee and expand their tastes, to stroll in the park, to visit the zoo, libraries, museums, and department stores. When they joined the predominantly Yankee and urban Congregational church in Watertown, Alex and Flora symbolically distanced themselves from their immigrant farm background. At the same time, their photographs document success—symbolized in the abundance of material goods, the handsome set of china, the Edison phonograph, the new Fords and Chevrolets. Alex recorded Milwaukee street scenes as well as Watertown celebrations and trips to visit relatives

in Iowa or friends in Madison. Visits to Henry and May in Milwaukee were "great for anything of educational value." It was there, at a local fair, that they saw their first movie, *The Great Train Robbery*.

The birth of a first child was often the event that plunged a family into photography.[4] The twins, Jennie and Edgar Krueger, were born on March 31, 1899. In numerous photos, Alex sentimentalized the innocence of childhood, a common theme in Victorian popular art and literature. As toddlers, Edgar and Jennie were photographed wearing matching overalls or suits, posed with the props of an idyllic childhood: calves and kittens, china dolls, toys, and Christmas trees. Shirley remarked: "I sometimes think my dad and Aunt Jennie were kind of spoiled children. I think they were quite a novelty, the twins." They played baseball with cow pies for bases; they were surrounded with pet guinea

Edgar and Jennie mimic their grandfather's catch. WHi(K91)200

65

pigs, rabbits, mice, gophers, baby raccoons, squirrels, and the usual assortment of farm dogs and cats. They shot sparrows and rodents with a slingshot, and later with an air rifle. (They brought their prey to the milkhouse, where grandfather August recorded the kill and rewarded them with a penny for each mouse or sparrow—and two cents for a rat.) The twins learned to milk the cows when they were nine, and in 1909 they received the first of many calves they were to raise. The Kruegers also drew on modern notions of child rearing. They adopted new strategies such as a weekly allowance and a children's savings account—following advice transmitted in the popular magazines of the day.

Life-cycle transitions spurred this fascination with family identity and change expressed in the photographs: with the birth of Alex and Flora's twins, there were four generations living together on the family farm. The extended family living together on the farm that they celebrated was, itself, a reflection of the bourgeois ideal of family ties that, according to historian Stephen Ruggles, led in the late nineteenth century to a rise in extended family households among the American middle class.

The Kruegers shaped their family story—an immigrant past followed by prosperity and local recognition—into an optimistic, future-oriented American epic. Their representations of themselves in photographs and stories were inextricably tied

Why do families go to such trouble to orchestrate these scenes? Anson Goetsch's mother reaches out to hold the hand of the youngest of her eight children. The sharply bent elbow and hand stiffly on the waist draw the eye to the older woman in the Krubsack family group similarly lined-up on their porch but with an uncooperative dog and lamb. The familiar animals suggest a natural informality in farm family life which turn-of-the-century city dwellers only experienced during brief excursions to the country or in longer respites at a summer cabin. WHi(X3)38082 (top) and WHi(K8)32

to various middle-class American ideals: success, self-improvement, abundance, sincerity, and domesticity. Alex and Flora Krueger, buoyed by good economic times, envisioned themselves as a mainstream American family. Their farm improvements reflected a broader concern for scientific solutions to problems of production applied to business and, increasingly, in the home. In their domestic consumption of furniture, china, clothing, and other goods, the Kruegers paralleled their urban counterparts.

Although theirs was not an isolated, ethnic world, the family farm and networks of kin continued to define the Kruegers' lives, in contrast to those who lived in city and village. The priority of farm needs

over domestic consumer goods would limit their participation in mainstream consumer culture during hard times. Their experience was also different from that of the urban middle class with its sharp distinction between home and the public world, and between women's and men's roles. Farm families retained economically productive work at home in the nineteenth century after urban men had followed their traditional skills from the home to the factory or office, and middle-class women had become increasingly isolated in the home. Gender divided work and decision-making on the family farm, yet women shared in the most grueling farm chores as well as caring for children and keeping house.

Between 1905 and 1920, the group living together on the Krueger family farm shrank from an extended family of nine to a nuclear family of three, and from three households to one. As the Kruegers prospered, these dramatic shifts were recorded in family photographs. With his brothers and sisters, August posed for a mourning photograph on the

The informality of these photographs from the Milwaukee Uttecht family collection capture a spontaneous gaiety of the event in contrast with Alex Krueger's stiff poses and Willie Buelke's careful compositions. With the advent of roll film, family photography would move away from carefully constructed images characteristic of the individual glass-plate negatives. WHi(X91)20678 (left) and WHi(X91)20677

porch of the log house. In 1913, the log house that had been William's retirement home was torn down. After August and Mary moved to Watertown, the original *Fachwerk* house stood empty for fifteen years. Jennie Krueger met her future husband, Ernst C. Breutzman, in 1916, when the Kruegers hired him to help at threshing time. While they courted in the shadow of World War I, both Ernst and Jennie, dressed in his navy uniforms, clowned for the camera. They were married in November, 1920, lived in Watertown, and later moved to Milwaukee where Ernst worked as an accountant. The next generation on the farm, Edgar and Elna Krueger's children, arrived simultaneously with the Great Depression. After 1930, the family photographs became sparser. They portray a family that weathered hard times well, but had little opportunity for travel, leisure or consumer pursuits.

Meaning in Family Photographs

Anson Goetsch described the artifice that went into one of Alex's photographs:

Alex used to take photographs at family reunions. I think he had some kind of rig in the camera that he could get in on the picture and pull a string or something and snap it with him in the picture.... He tried to have everybody look natural as could be.

In the 1890s, as many middle-class Americans took up amateur photography, picture-making became an opportunity to play with roles, rules, and sentiment—and thus offered the opportunity to become more consciously aware of what seemed natural in familial and social expectations. In photography, individuals articulated personal renditions of mores, consumerism, popular pursuits, and ideas about themselves in visual form. Alex and his cohort of family photographers found that they could preserve and yet differentiate themselves from their family identity in their photographs.

The photographic output of the three cousins—

Rexford Krueger was more successful than Alex at capturing moods and feelings, as in this photograph of his future wife Winifred Evans. However, the Kruegers and Buelkes were critical of his stylish soft focus, deep shadows, and framing which cropped tops of heads or hands. WHi Lot 3994/204

68

Alex Krueger, Willie Buelke, and Rexford Krueger—represents the range and diversity of family photography in the early twentieth century. While Alex framed the image from behind the camera, his subjects broke with everyday occupations to pose, often stiffly, facing the camera (and future viewers). By contrast, his cousin Willie Buelke "snapped" more spontaneous shots with his 5x7 format camera. Trained in a portrait studio, a detour on his way to farming, Willie may have been more comfortable with the equipment and processes. His snapshots were more informal than Alex's studio-like family groups; Willie approached the subject more intimately and was less concerned than Alex with symmetrical poses and carefully centered framing. Buelke's subjects seem more relaxed as well; his portraits of his parents with their grandchildren convey a sense of family affection. Martha Buelke seems at home with the cow she milked twice each day, and larger groups seem to cluster spontaneously, as though the picture-taking had only briefly interrupted the flow of conversation.

The Kruegers' younger cousin Rexford took up photography as a boy and by his early teens, perhaps inspired by his cousin Willie, he had set up as a professional photographer. In 1909, he wrote his aunt, "Dear Aunt Bertha, I am now very busy with my school work, music, and photography. I often think of the good times I had at your place last summer...." Rexford was more aware of the status of photography as both a popular hobby and an artistic endeavor.

The Kruegers' Iowa cousins remember with a great deal of humor Rexford, the city boy, and his frequent summer visits:

He used to about drive my Dad up the wall. He would

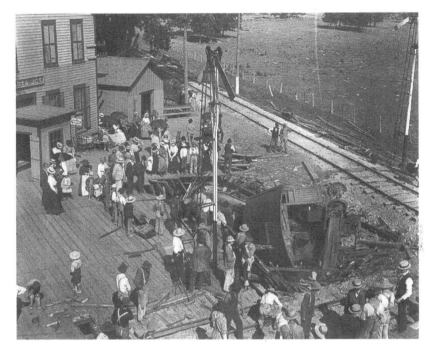

Disasters, reflecting a popular predilection for the unpredictability of modern life, were frequent subjects of amateur and commercial photography—as well as family stories. Willie Buelke may have seen a profit in the sale of photographs of this particular train wreck. WHi(B91)20

stay all summer and he would take pictures most all the time.... You know how farmers are—there's no time to pose and he always thought we had to pose.

Rexford, the boy photographer, created a record of rural life in Iowa. However:

...the last few times he [Rexford] came here he wasn't so much trouble 'cause he'd always be over to Evanses.... He found a girl that he wanted ... the Evans girls were all nice girls and it was a place to get rid of him to.

Winifred Evans Krueger recalled:

I remember the first time I saw Rexford. Berries used to grow wild along the roads and we used to have a regular

Confirmation in the church was considered a rite of passage and their father carefully composed portraits of the twins with symbols of their maturing gender roles to record the moment. Jennie was photographed with her hair down and the comb and brush set she received as a gift. WHi(K91)420

berry picking. I was with my sisters and Rexford came. He was just a little kid and I was barefooted. I knew he was a city boy and I tried to hide my bare feet because they said, 'Oh! Here comes Aunt Bertha and that fellow from Milwaukee.'

In 1909, he photographed Winnie's family and farm. By 1915, Rexford and Winnie were making captioned photograph albums and courting seriously. They were married in 1918 and went to live in Milwaukee.

The more conventional family photographers were sometimes lukewarm about Rexford's concerns with soft focus, shadows, and similiar "artistic effects," as shown in the album he and Winnie made during their courtship. His collection includes more artistic—and seemingly spontaneous or even covertly captured—scenes; his portraits and interiors use lighting to flatter the subjects; his "casual" groupings of people are in fact carefully arranged. Rexford invested in more elaborate equipment, kept up with new techniques through clubs and publications, and even exhibited his own work in photo club shows. In the 1920s and 1930s his interest in "pictorialism" grew and he took part in photographic salons and contests. His prize-winning photo of a railway engine with billowing plumes of steam reflects the influence of Edward Steichen and other photographic artists. It was shown, his widow recalled, in at least fifteen exhibitions. Shirley remarked that her grandfather, who drew on popular conventional subject matter, "didn't have a high regard for Rexford's photos because his [Alex's] idea

of a good picture was somebody standing there in their Sunday best in perfectly sharp focus."

The subjects of the photographs reflect and reaffirm attitudes and values. For example, Alex made a carefully matched pair of portraits of Jennie and Edgar at the time of their confirmation at the Congregational church in Watertown. The props in these coming-of-age photographs reveal popular early-twentieth-century notions about womanhood and manhood. Jennie is shown with mirror, brush, and comb, her hair let down. Such pictures of women were relatively common. Although she

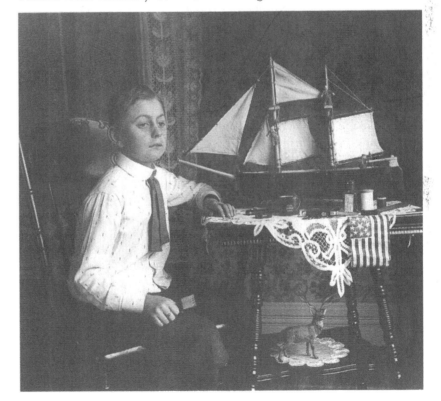

In his portrait, Edgar poses with male accouterments. Subsequent photographs in the sequence indicate that the formal picture-making became a playful family event as the twins, their mother, and aunt took up mock poses, peeking out from behind lace curtains. WHi(K91)419

might later become a farm wife with her hair fastened up, working in the fields, the picture focuses on her "crowning glory," her hair—symbol of her femininity and physical attractiveness. Edgar's picture, on the other hand, depicts him with the boat August had made for him years before. It also shows the tools and materials Edgar used to repair and refinish the boat, as if to demonstrate the skills Alex thought a man should have.

Family photographs may appear self-contained, a story within a frame; yet there is a great deal that goes on outside the frame. The viewer brings personal experience and associations to the image. Today, for example, family historians are encouraged to preserve the "artistic," meaning those spontaneous, sometimes accidental shots of blurred, moving figures; but to Alex Krueger, these were mistakes, which he likely culled from his negative collection. When we compare Alex Krueger's work to popular art and to other photographs of the early twentieth century, it becomes clear that his sentimental pictures of children, like "A Full Dozen," and his photographs of the marshy stream, with his family in their best outfits pretending to fish, were

also "artistic" creations in their own way. His son Edgar has firmly forgotten those afternoons spent posing in frilly shirts; instead, he recalls fishing with hooks made of bent pins, and how he and his sister feared that pickerel, with their sharp teeth, might bite them—appropriately down-to-earth memories for a boy who was about seven years old when the pictures were taken.

In still more overtly "invented" photographs, Alex captured humorous dress-up scenes, costume parties, and tableaux vivants ("living pictures" of people posed in scenes drawn from history, literature, and the arts). In the 1890s, these were all the rage, and photographers all over the country were making pictures of cultural subjects with titles like "Greek Statues" and "Romeo and Juliet." Patriotic and historic scenes—for example "Martha Washington's Tea Party"—were even more popular.

Such pictures held appeal for Alex Krueger, who was interested in his region's pioneer past and took photographs of surviving split-rail fences and settlers' cabins. In 1908, Alex, his sister Sarah, wife Flora, daughter Jennie, and cousin Tillie Volkman made their own history pictures. They got out the family treasures and spent afternoons dressed in

In composing portraits which demonstrate a pride in skills, family, and possessions, and in more intimate displays like these, the Kruegers and their peers became more consciously aware of the conventions regarding gender roles, as well as religious and social taboos. Dating from the 1890s, the photograph (near left) of his wife by Dr. Bass of Montello, Wisconsin, suggests both the pride and sensuality associated with a mature woman's unbound hair. Annie Sievers Schildhauer, an amateur artist and the wife of a civil official, photographed the everyday life of an urban, middle-class family including this humorous tableau. Such theatrical or fancy dress was a stock feature of social entertaining at the turn of the century, and frequently recorded in photographs. Women, in particular, were given a chance to play at exotic or exciting roles together with their female friends. WHi(K91)188 (far left), WHi(B35)98 (left), and WHi(X3)29519

costume in the barn, play-acting William and Wilhelmina's arrival from Pomerania before the camera. Inspired by a similar photograph their friend Kate Renk had sent them, some of the Krueger women posed as Pomeranian peasants spinning wool and mending clothes. Alex made photographs as a means of creating a historical record of *Fachwerk* architecture and disappearing crafts. The young women who posed in his photos were of course merely play-acting in emulation of family elders such as Johanna Krueger and Charlotte Goetsch who really had possessed the skills to spin

yarn and weave cloth. Still, there was a serious side to these pleasant afternoons in front of the camera. By dressing up and posing for the camera, the Kruegers demonstrated to themselves, and to all those who might view the photographs, that they felt their past was of value, much as the wider history depicted in the museum displays Alex loved to visit.

The same young adults who created these immigrant tableaux rejected, or at least mocked, family conventions when the dress-up theme car-

ried through into joke photographs or humorous scenes, similar to the humorous stereograph series marketed in the late nineteenth century. In the 1890s, as many middle-class Americans took up amateur photography, picture-making became an opportunity to play with roles, rules, and sentiment,

In cross-dressing and mugging for the camera, the Krueger family cousins playfully challenged or parodied both social distinctions and expectations for behavior. Alex Krueger produced many such pictures as postcards (most frequently featuring women dressed as men), including Hattie Fels Owen as "The Dude." WHi(B91)424 (left) and WHi(K91)473

and thus an opportunity to become more consciously aware of familial and social expectations. In two photographs, Alex combines peasant dress with "cross-dressing," his wife and sister alternately playing the role of male. The Krueger collection contains many other portraits of women wearing men's suits, smoking cigars, or riding horses—as well as a few photographs of men in women's dresses or hats. (The playing with gender roles implicit in such cross-dressing photography was not unusual for the period; it is evident in many extant photographic collections and albums.) In a group effort, Willie Buelke and the Kruegers staged and photographed several scenes of family members drinking whiskey and playing cards. They even made double exposures

showing one man playing against himself. Such photographs carry an unmistakably "naughty" or provocative message. As a Baptist cousin from Iowa remarked, looking at the photograph, "Oh! That was to torment someone!"

Family photographs gather meaning from the way families use them. Shortly after a picture is taken, the family audience uses the photograph as a record of a specific event, individual, or object. It becomes part of the family's communication network. The family sends copies of the photographs

Alex Krueger staged a tribute to the family's immigrant past with the series of photographs in Pomeranian peasant garb. Sarah and Flora spoof those same dress-up pictures when Flora dresses as a man. WHi(K91)401 (left) and WHi(K91)404

Rexford Krueger demonstrated his talent for conventional family portraiture in this photograph capturing the similarities of dress and demeanor and the easy relationship between his urban father Henry and his uncle August, a retired farmer. WHi Lot 3994/174

by mail or passes them around at get-togethers to let relatives who were absent catch up on family news. But older photographs frequently carry different, less specific meanings, even when the details of the subjects they picture are known. It becomes more important to know how someone looked when they were young than it is to recall particular events; to recall "how we went on picnics then.... [We] just threw everything in the car and went off." In later use, the Krueger children and grandchildren have found a different kind of affirmation—evidence of family continuity and heritage—in the same images.

The output of other family photographers shows the pervasive use of family photographs—tucked into the margins of dresser mirrors or crowding walls and mantels. For example, Theodore Faville, like Alex Krueger and Willie Buelke, photographed his family at home in La Crosse, Wisconsin, and his grandparents' home in Janesville in the late 1890s. The son and grandson of Wisconsin Congregationalist ministers, Theo (or Ted) was later superintendent of the Wisconsin Congregational Conference. Through the layering of images and objects from the simple and ubiquitous rocking chairs, a casual hammock, a flag draped from and partially concealing a pipe, a worn hat, a fan, and numerous small American flags, the Favilles fostered an intimate, familial sensibility in their family cottage, "Grand Haven." The objects, like the images, are souvenirs that remind and restate the family's satisfaction in their pursuits. The visual and material symbols validate or lend a sense of history to the contemporary family by making personal connections over time and distance.

In photographs, families gave tangible form to their sense of themselves and their aspirations. At the same time, the subject and the photographer could poke fun at themselves. As a niece wrote to her uncle, August Krueger:

Well, here I am now. Don't I look cross. I don't know what was the matter with me the day I had this taken. This

Inspired by commercial images, amateurs including the Krubsacks (top) created humorous scenes for the camera like this one of a "treed raccoon." An Iowa cousin remarked that "They were trying to torment someone," when the Krueger cousins made a series of double exposures which parodied Baptist strictures against playing cards, drink, and tobacco. WHi(K8)60 (top) and WHi(K91)393

is my first trial in developing and finishing, so you can't expect anything different.... You better all shut your eyes when you look at this picture.

Thus did individuals articulate personal renditions of mores, consumerism, popular pursuits, and ideas about themselves in visual form.

Postcards: Here We Are, What Do You Think Of Us?

Working in a makeshift closet darkroom, Alex and Sarah contact-printed glass-plate negatives onto commercially produced photographic postcard stock. With Willie Buelke, Rexford Krueger, and other friends and relatives, they began an intensive exchange of snapshots and messages that followed family networks to Chicago, Nebraska, California, and Alabama. (Alex's father August, and his uncles, Henry, William, and Albert, competed to see who could fit more words on their cards; their messages, written in tiny, spidery letters, often in German, are almost indecipherable.) The exchange of images and messages reached a peak between 1905 and 1915 when even the most mundane scenes became excuses for correspondence.

If stereoscopes were the high point of parlor entertainment and self-education, postcards were the most popular form of the souvenir craze of the day. Improvements in transportation and the success

These images from another Wisconsin family suggest the significant part photographs played when families articulated their sense of identity through domestic objects. The cabin interiors exhibit the family in the unpretentious intimacy of their leisure time, when conventions and formality could symbolically give way to the sincerity of casually placed wood furnishings and rag rugs. In this setting, photographs and memorabilia testify to a deep and spontaneous affection which the Faville family wanted to see in themselves. WHi(F3)90 (top) and WHi(F3)89

of that industry's promotion of every sort of travel fed the craze. Changes in postal regulations made correspondence by "penny postcard" a part of every trip. Photo postcards allowed any small town attraction to have cards of its own. The craze left us with some of the most interesting images of the period. The photographers who made them were part of a major industry that made cards for every taste and selected subjects designed to attract attention and impress. Their images offer a comprehensive catalog of what was considered up-to-date, humorous, dramatic, cozy, or beautiful by creator, sender, and recipient.

Families too could make cards of their own events to be shared and remembered. Store-bought postcards influenced the subject matter and style of the amateur postcards as the amateurs experimented with decorative masking paper to frame faces in hearts and ovals, posed children in sentimental scenes with baby animals, hand-tinted photographs to resemble lithographs, or hurried out to photograph the scene of a train wreck or natural disaster. Family groups and friends posed for each other in elaborate gags, which were mailed along with images of grand new buildings, shimmering lakes, and bustling main streets. "Who did they send the postcards to?" joked Anson wonderingly. "I know we got our share!"

Before the telephone, postcards and letters were "the next best thing to being there." Communication is an essential part of any network and, as the postcard craze caught up the Kruegers, they—along with the Buelkes, the Renks, the Goetsches, and other friends and relatives—exchanged homemade postcards as well as store-bought images of local monuments, accidents, and giant cabbages. For example, on a joke postcard depicting an automobile

Amateur photographers adopted the genre of the idyllic scene from both the Pictorialist movement in art photography and the growing belief in the health and psychological benefits of outdoor recreation, promoted most visibly by Theodore Roosevelt. Willie Buelke's version of fishing on the Rock River was printed on postcard stock. WHi(B91)265

chase to lasso a giant hare, Henry Krueger wrote his nephew Alex, "Your horses run fast, but I think the auto on the other side runs faster. Now I have answered your postal which I never received. Write soon." Other postcards showed their pride in "a full-blooded Holstein cow" or "the mother with her five colts, three matched teams." Some gossiped about beaux; others enumerated the harvest, announced a birth, or mourned a death. The cousins shared their recent photographic efforts, pointing out new techniques, bragging about new equipment, and praising each others' "snaps." The correspondence traced the lines of family and friendship networks to Milwaukee, Chicago, Iowa, Nebraska, Alabama, and California. The images they made, carefully

assembled in postcard albums, constitute a tangible record of the individual's place in the family network.

Photographs encompassed the dynamic tension that families faced: the new media was a vehicle for family continuity and tradition as well as a symbol of breaking new ground. As they engaged in picture-making, the Kruegers further integrated the family into the mainstream of American popular taste and consumer patterns while seizing this expressive medium to represent themselves as

Amateurs imitated their commercial counterparts in other ways. Each autumn while the twins were young, Alex staged a Christmas greeting produced as a postcard—a precursor to the Kodak family portrait. This one from 1908 bore the title "A Christmas Smile." Mocking the conventional image of "the family at home," Albert Goetsch posed with four of his children outside a shed. "This is on our new farm. Such is life," was the joking caption—with a biting edge—alluding to the family's difficulties in getting ahead. The Kruegers' neighbor, Alex Scholz, was an amusing local character—much like Edgar's own cousin Anson Goetsch—who trained animals for the entertainment of family and friends. The docile bull made for a clever postcard in the style of "Jackalopes" and giant vegetables—standard jokes of commercial postcard photographers. WHi(K91)497 (top), WHi(X3)37762 (left), and WHi(K91)542

special. Ordinary people had the means to represent themselves much as they had the means to acquire new products such as automobiles. In family photography, we can distinguish the contradictory impulses of mass culture towards both homogeneity and democratization.

Photography was a family affair. Both a hobby and a strategy for maintaining family ties, it was transmitted from one generation to the next. As people changed places while making photographs, other relatives must have operated Alex's camera. The children pitched in when it came to hand-tinting photographs, and Jennie Krueger—

pictured holding a camera about the time of her confirmation—took up the hobby as well. Shirley Krueger Oestreich began making photographs while she was attending the Dodge County Normal School, a local teachers' college, in 1949. Using one of her grandfather's cameras, she took all the usual pictures: classmates, a trip to Washington, a school initiation. When she had children of her own, Shirley began taking pictures of them. Today there are photographers throughout the Krueger family. Some, like Shirley's son Glenn, who has a serious interest in photography, use the camera in pursuit of a specific subject; for example, he mainly takes pictures of railroads and trains. But most Kruegers make pictures of family activities for that old and time-honored purpose: "remembrance."

Heat and moisture crackled the surface of Willie Buelke's negatives, stored for years in a shed along with old farm equipment and other relics of vanished handicrafts. His domestic interiors, including this portrait of his father August holding his grandson Lester, reveal a family firmly embedded in the popular consumer patterns of the time. Willie may also have taken this view of his cousins Alex and Sarah, out picture-taking in the countryside. WHi(B91)386 (left) and WHi(X3)37815

EXPANDING HORIZONS

ALTHOUGH they owned a half-share in the family dairy operation, Alex and Flora were looking at opportunities to buy land in 1902 when he visited a cousin, Paul Goetsch, in Shelby County, Alabama. Alex, traveling with his Uncle Ernst Goetsch, looked over the area but returned home dismayed by the state of southern agriculture—"at least fifty years behind Wisconsin," as he recounted. However, he brought back photographs and stories of farmers working with oxen, whole tenant families arduously picking cotton by hand, black women tending white children, old slave quarters, and dusty small towns with pigs rooting in the gutters. Although he looked reasonably prosperous posing with his family for Alex's camera, Paul Goetsch later moved back to Wisconsin as well. Like Paul, the family's widening networks of kin served as resources and outposts for new opportunities and occupations.

Farm and family, family and kin: all were interconnected. The Kruegers' ubiquitous "four generation" photographs reflect the enduring pull of family and descent among the strands that made up the family's sense of identity in the early twentieth century. The Kruegers innovated against this background of traditions rooted in their Pomeranian immigrant experience and shaped by their drive for family economic security. Traditional ways of doing things, and of viewing the world, operated both as constraints and as strategic resources as the family adapted to dramatic economic and material changes. The role of the extended family, as well as the cooperation between generations on the family farm, were instrumental in the family's adaptation to mainstream developments. Locational stability characterized German immigrant settlement areas, but economic security and the maintenance of the family depended on improving the farm and transmitting it undivided from one generation to the next, forcing siblings to look for cheap land elsewhere or for new economic opportunities. In time, traditional farming methods were replaced by new machinery and equipment, family enterprise was supplemented by cooperative enterprises, local markets gave way to national and international markets, and churches divided into factions—often as a result of tensions between old ways and new.

Alex recorded a trip he and his uncle made to Alabama in 1902 to check out agricultural conditions and opportunities. He was clearly intent on documentation when he captioned this photograph: "A typical 'Negro' home of Shelby Co., Alabama. Colored family and house.... The house was occupied by two families, 14 total people." WHi(K91)233

Main streets everywhere were powerful symbols of progress for commercial and manufacturing centers. Paving gave an "up-to-date" look and local businessmen must have hoped that such visible progress would attract new customers. Pharmacist and professional postcard photographer, Henry F. Bergmann, captured this important change to Watertown's Main Street, which, for the Kruegers and their neighbors, was the gateway to a wider, rapidly changing world. WHi(B61)124

Pressures for land or employment took family members out of the local community. In succeeding generations, young men and women both set out to provide for themselves. Movement and change meant taking risks; but at the same time the younger generation tried to minimize the risk by using reports from their relatives or friends to check out the glowing accounts of boosters, promoters, and land agents. As individuals and family groups moved outward, they often relied on relatives who

had preceded them. They, in turn, opened opportunities for younger siblings and cousins. Cousins exchanged information on new agricultural methods and took advantage of networks of kin to make their way in the world. In recent years, pieces of the same networks have provided family members with a sense of continuity in the face of new developments requiring new adaptive strategies.

William E. Goetsch described his own experience as a second child and "the farm of his Father only ninety acres of which eighteen acres was marshland." With not enough work for the five brothers, William set off at age sixteen "to padel his own way," as he put it. Still, he was hardly alone when he set out to work as a farm laborer near Chicago. His cousin, another Bill Goetsch, alerted him to the opportunity in the big city and promised his father to watch out for young William as his "gardeen" (guardian). Later, his brother Henry urged William to come north to Racine, Wisconsin, where he could secure a job as a clerk: "It was easier than working on a Farm and I would not be lonesome." His departure raised the problem of how to collect his full pay from an unsuspecting employer; his cousin advised him "to git my pay for the time I had been there and skip— he would." To allay suspicions, Bill told his boss he needed money for new boots and overalls:

He gave me a due bill on the Station Store [instead of cash] and told me to put the Sadel on Fanny and ride to the Station and git what I need. Now what to do I did not know.... The train leaves for Chicago 8 a.m. It was about 7 o'clock when I started so I thought I will go and bid my cousin William good-by. It was about one mile north from the Station when I got there my boss was coming horseback looking for me. I ran in the Barn and Cousin Bill covered me with a fork full of hay.

Once he got to Racine, Henry provided the information and support that a newcomer needed. William recorded Henry's first remarks: "How do you feel you look very thin and your hair is so long we will have to go to a barbershop you have to git your hair cut and change your boots, I have a pair they will just fit you. This is different then in the country you have to dress better. I have a place for you in a flour, feed & grocery Store on 6th street. Brace up and walk straight. I suppose you are hungry." In short, William did not "padel his own way" without crucial advice and material assistance from family members.

Those who made the right choices often started a new chain of movement or the more widespread adoption of new strategies. In the process, networks of rural neighborhood, ethnicity, kin, and church changed, fragmented, and widened.

The Local Scene

In geographic and political terms, the Krueger farm was at the core of concentric circles of social interaction, surrounded first by their rural neighborhood and township and then by Dodge County with its county seat in Juneau and its economic hub in nearby Watertown.[1] These geographic rings were intercut by dynamic, interlocking personal networks of kin, church, ethnicity, and business that ebbed and flowed over time according to family interests, personal affinities, and economic developments. Living within view of Watertown, the Kruegers often had business or visited with relatives and friends in town. But they remained a rural

family with friends and kin across the countryside. They helped their neighbors with farm work, participated in township government, joined volunteer associations, and helped found organizations to market their products.

Nearby urban centers provided an immediate arena in which young adults experimented with occupations and sometimes established businesses. When the Kruegers arrived at Sugar Island in 1851, Watertown was the nearest metropolis and the state's second-largest city. Its growth had slowed after the 1870s as the rest of the region developed, but it remained the most important city between Milwaukee and Madison, the state capital. New ideas and new products flowed from these urban centers to

Streets were not paved in the commercial center of Watertown when August was a young farmer and his brother-in-law, William E. Goetsch, was trying his hand at commerce. Courtesy of the Watertown Historical Society

85

William and his two brothers opened a dry-goods store in Watertown with financial help from their parents. A few years later the partnership was dissolved and William and his wife Bertha made their way to Iowa. WHi(X3)38111

alert, outward-looking people like the Kruegers who subscribed to a Milwaukee newspaper and two Watertown papers.

The cluster of buildings centered along the main streets and squares of small cities and towns testified to the factors that united the countryside. In the 1880s, Watertown's city directory boasted:

Six dry-goods stores, eleven groceries, two drug stores, three hardware stores, two bakeries, three meat markets, two livery stables, a tobacconist, seven blacksmiths, six wagon and two cabinet shops, two jewelry stores, fourteen shops, one chair factory, one machine and five shoe shops, one fork and hoe, one plow, one door and sash and one salaratus [sic] factory,

three flouring and four sawmills, one fanning mill and two harness making shops, two book stores, one gunsmith, one tannery, one furnace, one pottery, one carding machine, one oil mill, one rake and cradle [scythe] factory, one woolen and yarn factory, two printing offices, six schoolhouses, two select schools and one bank.*

These businesses and organizations offered entertainment, markets, services, and the credit and products necessary for a successful farm operation.

Farmers were drawn to Watertown by commerce, associations, and celebrations like the Fourth of July fireworks on Concordia (later Tivoli). The urban center brought farm families in contact with outsiders; for example, Edgar recalled his apprehensions about gypsies who made camp near his farm and sold horses at the monthly market:

They would doctor those horses up. They were outlaws oftentimes. Something was wrong with them oftentimes, with the horses.... Well, it was hard to tell; they looked good at the fair.

However, Watertown maintained its distinctly German character in the *Viehmarkt* or monthly cattle fair, in newspapers like the *Weltbürger* ("English and German job printing")—a Democratic, German-language weekly—its German "opera societies," secret societies, bowling clubs, and literary societies, and ethnic organizations like the *Turnverein, Deutscher Krieger Verein, Liederkranz,* and *Plattdeutscher Verein* (a German social and insurance organization, largely for farmers, with its own hall in Watertown). On May 13, 1881, the *Watertown Gazette* reported that the Germans' springtime favorite, dark bock beer, "is doing its work at the present time." William Hartig, brewer and malt-ster, ran an advertisement on every other page of the 1900-1901 Jefferson County directory. Watertown took pride in its local German specialty. "What they always talked about was the stuffed goose," meaning the famous geese that were force-fed special noodles to produce enlarged livers. In 1898, the *Watertown Daily Times* announced "Annual May Ball at the Turner Opera House, Saturday, May, 14. Admission 50 cents." And in 1908, the paper notified citizens of the twenty-third annual dance of the *Plattdeutscher Verein*:

Sloan's full orchestra will furnish the music for dancing. The annual dances given by this society are always looked forward to with anticipation, as a good time is always in store for those who attend.

The Kruegers seized some of these opportunities. August joined the *Plattdeutscher Verein* and took his family to hear Robert M. La Follette, William Jennings Bryan, and other populist-progressive politicians at the Turner Hall in Watertown. The Baptist and later the Congregational churches brought them to town on Sundays. Alex played for a baseball team in Watertown and the family brought their Fourth of July picnic to Tivoli Park to watch the fireworks. Elna Sommerfield and Edgar Krueger met after her uncle found work for her at a local college. Women gained some economic independence by selling eggs and other farm produce at the monthly market.

Legal business took farmers to the county seat in Juneau where the Kruegers visited Mary's family, the Goetsches. Mary's sister Martha Sara Goetsch married August Buelke, a carpenter and farmer. August was "a confirmed Baptist" and was sought out from miles around for his interpretations of the scriptures. (Oddly, for the man was also known as the black sheep of the family.) The Buelkes moved twenty miles away to a farm on the outskirts of Juneau. Martha, August, and their three children, Ida, William (Willie), and Ernest (Ernie) were popular with the Krueger family. The county seat offered some entertainment: "On Saturday nights," Anson Goetsch recalled, "we would walk all the way to the depot and watch who came and who left; then, there was always a band concert that they had on Saturday nights." Extended family exposed the cluster on the farm to new hobbies, including photography, and to new economic strategies as Willie and Ernie tried on different occupations, from mail carrier and professional photographer to schoolteacher. They visited back and forth between the two farms frequently for Sunday dinners or picnics, sometimes traveling by train the short distance between Watertown and Juneau.

For the first generation, the brief period of formal schooling rarely took children beyond the rural neighborhood. William E. Goetsch described the childhood of his wife, Bertha Krueger, when her family "owned a little track of eighty acres mostly marsh and swamp." As he said:

There was not much tillable land to make more money than just a scant living and the nearest School House was 5 miles distant, with 4 months school in the year. So, you see, you could not expect much of an education for a little girl. To walk 5 miles in stormy weather, she could not attend. And in the month of March she had to help with making Sugar and Maple Syrup.

August and Mary's children graduated in the 1880s from eighth grade at the nearby one-room schoolhouse. "Country school," Edgar observed, "went only to the ninth grade, then you graduated and you were lucky if you even got that far—you went maybe to the sixth grade and that was it." However, there was dramatic change: Henry graduated from the state teachers' college in Whitewater; August enrolled in a four-month accounting course at Northwestern University in Watertown; Alex briefly attended high school in Watertown and, following a path already taken by another uncle, he completed the agricultural short course at the University of Wisconsin in Madison.[2]

After clerking in Racine, William Goetsch and two of his brothers started a store in Watertown. He and Bertha Krueger, fellow church members and neighbors already related by marriage, were married in 1872; she was then nineteen and he was twenty-four. The first three of their seven children were born in Watertown. The store ledgers show that William's father was a good customer as well as a creditor. Although Bertha's brother August had met the responsibilities to his siblings set forth in the

contract with his father, he also helped his brothers-in-law, the Goetsches, with loans to their business. In 1872, August's account book shows loans to "Goetsch & Bros" of $500, of which $100 was loaned in three installments in a single day. Despite such family support, however, the enterprise foundered. There are conflicting explanations for the failure of the Watertown store; William blamed expansion and the resulting debt:

Father had a mortgage on a farm. He sold it and furnished us the money. It went fine. We had a big trade, till we went in to everything. [We] had to hire help, rent another building, and borrow money at the rate of 10%. Then I sold out. I went to Howard County, Iowa, bought me a Farm of 80 acres, and paid 1100 Dollars in cash.

Willie Buelke took a picture of his brother and fellow postal employees when Ernie took a job as a mail carrier with the Juneau post office. Another time, he used a small format camera to inconspicuously document a local farm auction. WHi(B91)202 (left) and WHi(B9)359

Anson Goetsch thought that the store succumbed to imprudent business practices, aquisitive competition among the brothers' wives—"if one got a fur coat, the others had to get one, too"—and the brothers' drinking habits. A cousin suggested that, after the store failed, Bertha brought the family to Iowa in order to get William away from Milwaukee, "where all that Milwaukee beer was." Others said that William just wanted to "roam."

In any case, urban centers provided outposts of opportunity for the sons and daughters of surrounding farms that also brought change to everyday life on the farm. Sarah Krueger lived with her parents, sharing Alex's photographic pursuits and working on the farm until marrying John Bhend on October 4, 1913, when she was in her late thirties. John, a cheese-maker, had been born in Switzerland. John and Sarah moved to Watertown, where he worked in real estate and construction. Rather than enjoying semi-retirement on the family farm, August and Mary Krueger moved to Watertown in 1913 as well. Alex and Flora signed a mortgage agreement with his parents and bought the farm for $6,000 on April 29, 1914. Still, August often walked out to the farm to lend a hand; and Sarah's two children, Irene and Marcel, spent part of each summer there.

The Kruegers sometimes envied town life. August's great grandson recalled that even in the 1940s the city offered so much, "but there was no way you could be there; it was always milking time six-thirty, you

Willie Buelke photographed many Juneau area businesses, their proprietors and employees. This picture is the interior of the brand-new store his cousin, Theodore Schwantz, rushed into completion just in time for the 1903 Christmas trade. The butcher displays the highest quality meat products. WHi(B91)152 (top) and WHi(B9)223

89

William and Bertha Goetsch's substantial second farm was far less rugged than their first, located out on "the Wild 80." WHi(B91)245

know." However, the focus for the family's social life remained kin, their ties to the Baptist church, and the neighborhood.

Out in Iowa

The expectations of mutual assistance—and the resulting tensions—structured Krueger family life well into the twentieth century. Family members understood whom they could depend on, where and who their kin were, where their loyalties and their responsibilities lay. People learned from and built their social lives around their relatives to an extent that created friction at the time and today might seem intrusive or burdensome. Of the bond between Mary Krueger and her sister Martha Buelke, Martha's grandson said, "they were so close, it felt just like home at the Kruegers'." Edgar Krueger commented in a similar vein on his extended family:

I think all those families, years ago, were kind of close-knit families. We all had a common interest; in fact, every-body working together knew what everybody else was doing, and everybody had something to say about it, too.

Reciprocity and mutual assistance came with intrusions into family decisions, resulting, at times in antagonism between kin even when they moved as far away as Iowa.

Mary and August Krueger's siblings and their families clustered, for the most part, around Watertown and Juneau in Wisconsin and near Lime Springs and Cresco in Iowa, a second node in the family network. The experiences of August's sister Bertha Krueger Goetsch and her family illustrate both the opportunities of outward migration and the impact of kin at home in Wisconsin. After the failure of the Watertown store, relatives helped William and Bertha follow other relatives to northern Iowa in search of land, family continuity, and the secure old age their parents had sought in Wisconsin.

In the Cresco area, the Krueger enclave blended into the local settlement of Germans and Welsh known as "Golden Ridge." William wrote:

I had a Family a wife one girl 2 boys and my good wife

Alex Krueger's hobbies of photography and genealogy combine in the caption for this portrait: "Wedding picture of Mr. Wm. Goetsch enlarged from small tintype March 1903. Mrs. Goetsch was Bertha Krueger, married William Goetsch, moved to Iowa." The couple celebrated their golden wedding anniversary in January, 1922, and later that spring visited their Wisconsin relatives where Alex photographed the celebration. WHi(K91)3 (left) and WHi(K91)449

worked hard. I was not discouraged. I was fond of hunting. One day I shot a big bobcat. She weighed 60 lbs. My neighbors called me Nimrod.

William, a n'er-do-well who preferred fishing and hunting to developing the family farm, left most of the work on Bertha's broad shoulders. William and Bertha came to Iowa with little capital; like her father in the years immediately following immigration, Bertha worked off the farm to bring in cash:

My grandmother worked for the neighbors, shocking oats and that sort of thing ... to earn some more money for the

family. Her children were real young and she just took them along and set them by ... and when she moved on down the field, I expect she would move the child from shock to shock actually.

Although William "could tell you yarns and stories that would rock you for a week," Bertha won fame for her hard work and survival skills. "Bertha could bake bread out of sawdust," people said. It was Bertha, a grandson related, who "really kept the ship of state steady."

The first farm was "starvation avenue." Lorena Goetsch Evans, a storyteller like William, recalled that the first years were a struggle for stability. "We were always called the poor Goetsches." Their Irish neighbors likely helped them avoid starvation and William tried to reciprocate:

We lived first down by the river on the 'Wild 80' before we moved over by Cresco. There were a lot of Irish [Catholics] out there and they were real good to us. Dad used to take us to their church but Ma was a strict Baptist and wouldn't go.

At her own daughter's prompting ("Tell her about the 'Wild 80.'... Tell her about the wolves."), Lorena, recalled the hazards of a frontier farm:

Ma and Pa were real poor when they came out here. They came in a covered wagon and they didn't have anything. Dad used to say, they lived the first few years on rabbits and good neighbors. The land there by the river was wooded

When asked to comment on this photograph of the Goetsch family at work stacking hay in August, 1909, a wide range of memories were recorded: Lorena Goetsch Evans remembered that her Welsh in-laws frowned on women working in the fields, while other Iowa relatives joked that their young city cousin, Rexford Krueger, was a lot of trouble because he always wanted them to stop work and pose for pictures. Still, they saved and valued the photographic record he made of summers on the Iowa farm. Flora, Mary, Edgar, and Jennie Krueger appear in another Iowa picture from the same year. WHi(X3)37836 (top) and WHi(X3)37837

and hilly. Ma took the wagon and the babies down to the river to do laundry one day and, coming back, the wheel hit a rock and stuck. Ma loosed the horse but she couldn't ride. She was going to leave the babies—it was, let's see, Edward and Minnie—asleep in the wagon while she ran back. But she picked them up and carried them back to the house leading that old horse. When they got back to the wagon, the blankets were all pulled out and torn in the

dirt. It was evening and they heard them that night—the wolves. There were wolves on the "Wild 80" back then.

William and Bertha sold the first farm and, with help from their family, purchased better land near Lime Springs, where they raised their seven children. After the move, life was still dangerous and demanding. In the end, the Goetsches prospered; the children bought farms nearby and "all the girls married farmers." In the afterglow of struggle was family pride. Lorena said, "We were always called the

Older cousins sneered at Rexford's photographs which reflected a contemporary spontaneity—such as this one of a calf sniffing the boy in the grass. On a 1910 visit to the Bigalk home in Cresco, Iowa, he took a funny version of a conventional house and family portrait. WHi Lot 3994/130 (left) and WHi(X3)38116

His Iowa cousins commented that they saw a lot less of Rexford once he met Winnie Evans. They courted for many years before they married and she joined him in Milwaukee. A more informal snapshot of Lorena, her husband, Herbert Evans, and their three daughters suggests the changes in image style and content that came with the use of roll film. WHi Lot3994/59 (left) and WHi Lot 4303/414

poor Goetsches, but we showed them [their relatives], we got them all beat."

Separated from both family and the Baptist church, they made concessions, attending the Catholic church a few times and later joining a nearby Methodist church as August and Martha Buelke had done when they moved from the Watertown area to Juneau in Wisconsin. However, they maintained the Baptist objections to cards, drink, and dancing, as well as the commitment to adult baptism by immersion. Lorena recalls the day she and her brother were baptized in the Iowa River:

Oh what a crowd! Great curiosity to see someone get baptized immersed. None of these Evangelicals believed in it. They were all sprinkled; that was enough.... But that was the way we believed; we believed in John the Baptist—it's right there in the Bible.... There was quite a few of them and one of them, one of the girls, she got clear down but her bangs stood up about this much out of the water. So they always said that the Devil was still in her hair!

William, a deacon in the local church, embarrassed Lorena after she married by coming to her husband's church: "They asked him to come and speak. Of course, he was a very strong Baptist. He had to bring that in.... That didn't go over good here at all because none of them believed in it." Grandchildren and great-grandchildren attended the local church but also turned to adult baptism; a grand-daughter-in-law was even "rebaptized" when she married into the family. A grandson explained, "They didn't believe in playing cards or dancing. They couldn't see themselves going to movies or to town Saturday nights."

William paralleled August and Henry Krueger's civic leadership and political independence. Lorena said of him, he "was a Democrat through and through; he couldn't say anything good about a Republican," and his grandchildren believed him "the only Democrat in Albion Township." William "liked to argue politics real well.... It would get a little loud; it just sounded like they were about to hit each other. But actually, it was just political." William and his son Edward supported the Democratic presidential candidate, "The Star of the West," William Jennings Bryan.

The Kruegers had moved to Iowa to join a cluster of Goetsch relatives, but they soon began to inter-marry with the local Welsh settlement: Amanda married Tom Thomas; Ed married Tom's cousin Pearl Evans; Lorena married Pearl's brother Herbert Evans; and William married the Evanses' cousin, Sylvia Grabau. Relatives joke that Tom Thomas was initially too shy to propose in person and, instead, proposed on the telephone—to which Amanda responded, "Yes! [pause] Who is this?"

Education had proven a successful strategy for Henry and May Krueger in Wisconsin, and the frequent visits back and forth as well as postcards featuring his school and his impressive responsibilities as principal undoubtedly influenced his nephews and nieces. In addition, the Welsh neighbors and in-laws, who frowned upon women laboring in the fields, provided different models for women's roles and occupations.

Like several of the Evans daughters, Lorena wanted to be a schoolteacher; she recalled: "I was the first [Goetsch] that graduated from the stone schoolhouse—eighth grade. There was big doings down in Granger [a nearby town]." Lorena continued at a nearby school for five or six weeks, boarding in town with her father's cousin in exchange for butter and eggs. But the school was closed down for lack of pupils. After much pleading, Lorena recounted:

Rexford makes this 1911 portrait of his parents into a home-coming story. WHi Lot 3994/141

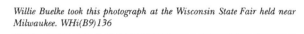

Willie Buelke took this photograph at the Wisconsin State Fair held near Milwaukee. WHi(B9)136

I was out in the field working—shockin' grain. When I came home I saw a truck there and a man and a woman and my mother and father standing there. Dad came to meet me, all smiles. He said, 'We've been waiting for you.... Come in the house. Something here I want to show you.' So we went in the house and [the woman] sat down to this old organ. Oh, she played so beautiful. He looked at me all smiles and said, 'How do you like it?' I said, 'I just love it.' He said, 'If you don't say anything more about going to school, I'll buy that for you.'

When they married, Lorena and her husband owned a trunk of clothes, a team of horses, and an organ. They rented two farms in succession before purchasing their own place in 1910. At age ninety-six, Lorena Evans was still capable of pumping out a familiar hymn, "Nearer My Lord to Thee," on the same organ.

By contrast, Lorena's brother, Edward Goetsch, graduated from the University of Northern Iowa in Cedar Falls, later earning a doctorate and the post of Iowa state superintendent of schools. Although he lived in Cedar Falls, Edward Goetsch also owned a nearby farm which his brothers worked in his absence. However, raised on the stories of Lorena's aspirations, her three daughters graduated from college.

City Cousins

Henry Krueger became the most cosmopolitan of William and Wilhelmina's six children. Following high school and a year at the Watertown Academy, he taught in rural schools for three years—earning, he said, "the munificent sum of twenty dollars a month" during his first term. His daughter-in-law recalled that he then earned his way through Whitewater Normal School (now the University of Wisconsin at Whitewater) by asking the school's president if he could work for his tuition and board at the president's home: "I want to go to school. I will work hard, I will live in the barn and take care of your horses." Summers, Henry helped with haying on the Krueger farm and worked on a crew draining marshes around Watertown.

How you meet your husband or wife tells something about the way you fit into society. The first generation Kruegers and Goetsches married neighbors and fellow church members. Later generations met spouses through family connections. Even when an occupation provided the introduction, kinship was often involved. For instance, Sarah's husband, John, a Swiss immigrant, was the brother of the cheesemaker at the Rock Cheese Factory. Henry was different; he met his wife at school, as many professionals do, and married his classmate, May Josephine Maxon, in 1881, the year after he graduated. However, their son Rexford followed the family pattern and married an Iowa neighbor and his cousin by marriage, Winifred Evans.

Henry and May were urban progressives, working to establish public playgrounds and organizing night school courses for adult immigrants in sewing and cooking, art and English. They pursued successful teaching careers in Milwaukee, where both eventually became principals. In addition, Henry was president of the Teachers' Retirement Fund Association and of the Principal's Association; he lobbied for the Milwaukee Permanent Tenure Office and Pension Fund Law in the Wisconsin legislature between 1903 and 1909. They were members of the First Unitarian Church of Milwaukee—a more dramatic break with Henry's Baptist upbringing than Alex and Flora's choice of the local Congregational church. Though Henry was an admirer of populist orator William Jennings Bryan, he also served as delegate to state Republican party conventions as a La Follette supporter.

During their first decades in Wisconsin, the Kruegers reached Milwaukee by way of a rough toll road constructed of planks. In the late nineteenth century, with the advent of an electric interurban train linking Watertown and Milwaukee, and of course later the automobile, Henry's home served as "outpost" for the extended family, opening up the possibility of city art and culture, fancy stores, and jobs. The exchange of visits and information flowed both ways—opening up new opportunities for rural cousins and permitting city relatives to renew ties to the family and to the increasingly sentimentalized associations with the pace and values of rural life. Henry, fond of outdoor life and sports, frequently brought his family out to visit his brothers and sisters in the Watertown area and in Iowa. They celebrated Thanksgiving and other holidays on the old family farm, and one summer they rented a nearby farmhouse. Henry and May felt a nostalgia for country life coupled with a belief in the healthful effects of fresh air and natural surroundings.[3] In 1908, Henry thanked William and Bertha:

I have been wanting to write to you for a long time to thank you for all that you have done for my boy Rexford. I

Although he availed himself of the newest photographic processes, Rexford composed this fairly conventional portrait of his extended family gathered around the dinner table. WHi(X3)38125

hope that some time I shall be able to repay you. It was just the right kind of treatment for Rexford. He seems to be over his nervousness.

Henry's Iowa relatives regularly took his sons off his hands for the summer, and the boys' holidays in the country also freed Henry and May to travel extensively on their own.

* * *

Family members used networks to acquire the tools, resources, and opportunities they needed to get things done. Taking and giving such aid built strong bonds of obligation with the expectation that the recipients would later reciprocate in kind.

Family relations were not without conflict; moves may have been precipitated by the desire for distance as well as the chance for new economic opportunities. It is clear from family accounts that William Goetsch found his brother-in-law August overbearing at times and may have been uncomfortable in proximity to his parents who had risked their farm on the brothers' failed store. Henry Krueger, a Republican insider, may have had trouble discussing politics with William, who "never saw a Republican he liked." Everyday relations were also the source of resentments; Lorena recalled that her aunt and uncle were regular Sunday dinner guests, invited or not: "Every Sunday, just as sure as four o'clock came, here came the Bigalks and stayed for supper." Sarah Krueger wrote home from Iowa that her Uncle Otto "looked as sour as a piss pot. He is too sober to be happy." Religious practices and beliefs were also a source of criticism from one generation to the next.

Modern life, which is said to have had so many corrosive effects on the mythic old extended family, actually has produced some benefits for family life. We live longer and more of us get to know our great-grandchildren or great-grandparents. Easy travel allows more visits between family members. Today, as in the past, when couples have children, the new parents turn more toward their kin, and it is not uncommon for a mother to fly great distances cross-country to help out with the birth of her daughter's child. Relying on family advice or assistance, individuals could minimize economic and personal risks as they tried out a new location or a new business like the Goetsch brothers' store in Watertown.

The Krueger and Goetsch families' horizons opened up as they followed networks of kin to nearby towns, cities, other states, and other countries. Herman Goetsch, Mary's brother, moved to Los Angeles with his family in 1905 and sent postcards encouraging his brothers and sisters to make a visit or to retire nearby in the warm, sunny climate. His son, Paul Goetsch, had earlier moved with his family to Alabama, only to return to Wisconsin. Alex's brother-in-law, William Wendorf, went off to Costa Rica to make his way as superintendent on a banana plantation. When he came home for a visit he clowned for Alex's camera wearing his tropical white suit in wintry Wisconsin; he also brought photographs of exotic-looking jungles, waterfalls, and people. A more distant cousin became a missionary and worked in Africa until the Boer War made German names like Krueger and Goetsch suspect to the British authorities. These networks of far-flung kin gave the family at home glimpses and experiences of new places through their letters and photographs.

At the core of the Krueger network were William and Wilhelmina's six children. The Kruegers' ties of kinship and friendship have radiated out from the home farm and rural neighborhood, forming a network of households and family groups scattered across the country. The family has maintained close ties through visits, reunions, mutual assistance, correspondence, and shared hobbies.

As the extended family spread and the older generation of siblings passed away, many of the old family networks dissolved and new ones emerged. Over the span of a century, the Kruegers have kept up close ties spanning generations and distant cousins. Through infrequent correspondence, the Kruegers in Wisconsin kept in touch with Old World relatives for even longer than that, and in recent years they have begun to renew these ties through family visits. Bob and Beatrice Krueger's home has recently served as an outpost for a young German cousin exploring opportunities in America.

Like many young Americans at the turn of the century, Alex and Flora's cousin Willie Wendorf went into the jungle seeking success. Willie became a superintendent on a Costa Rican banana plantation, where he lived with his wife and three children. During a 1904 Wisconsin winter visit, Willie posed in tropical dress with Alex. Willie soon returned to the plantation, but died there of fever some time later. WHi(K91)343 (left) and WHi(K91)333

IMMIGRANT STORIES
FAMILY AND MEMORY

WITH rich detail and carefully timed pauses, embellishments and repetition, a good storyteller can make a dramatic account out of "the time the goats ran away with the cart." The cracker-jack storytellers are often well-known family characters such as William E. Goetsch, who—I was told—would strike a comical pose with his lanky frame draped around a chair, "and then he would have another story." When he was done, Bill would always say, "By jingus, that sure is so!"

"Uncle Bill," a nephew said, "would embellish stories just a little—like 'how the West was won!'" Sons and daughters, themselves in their sixties, affirm their affection and respect for parents or older relatives by cajoling from them one more rendition of the day the house burned down: "Mother, remember, you were at the old stone school...." Through such mundane stories and recollections, families record the impact of migration, technological change, key characters, popular fads, and crucial historical developments. The event of telling, of reconstructing the past in the present, and the

role of the storyteller—these are frequently as important as the substance of the tale.

Alex Krueger's younger cousin, Anson Goetsch, was a well-liked character who, in the family parlance, could tell a yarn as easily as he could laugh at one told on him. Storytelling was as much a part of Anson's persona as his dogged determination to do things his own way, from his exploits as a lonely young cowboy in Montana to his stubborn attachment to mule teams, decades after his Wisconsin neighbors had replaced their horses with tractors. He trained performing mules, dogs, cats, horses, and chickens, and, with his wife Dorothy and their grandson, set out with a mule team in 1976 to go from Wisconsin to Washington, D.C., as part of an American Bicentennial wagon train. Anson talked in stories and it is hard to tell which came first, the stories or the character who told them.

The immigrant story that Anson Goetsch learned from his much older cousin Willie Buelke begins with a tragicomic conflict between two brothers and concludes with an unusual marriage.[1] According to the story, Anson's grandfather and his brother were in love with the same girl back in Germany: "There was a shortage of girls over there; so, they got into a terrible fight over that girl. Without telling each other, they were both supposed to leave for the

---

During interviews, Edgar Krueger frequently touched on a theme that was also evident in many of his father's photographs: that of a distinctive childhood growing-up among four generations. In 1904, Edgar and Jennie visit with their great-grandparents on the porch of the log house located across the road from the family farm. WHi(K91)198

United States." One brother dropped from sight in England; Anson's grandfather made his way to Wisconsin:

Then, he's supposed to have married a Chickataw [sic] Indian girl. Now, they were a civilized tribe; they lived East of the Mississippi River ... and we came to find out some of them in that tribe ... even had blue eyes. So that's how we claim that our great-grandma was a Chickataw Indian Princess.

The American Indians that Anson refers to—presumably a corruption of Choctaw and Chickasaw—were southeastern tribes which struggled to survive through accommodation with the surrounding European-American culture. They were forced west of the Mississippi when land-hungry plantation owners pressured Congress to pass the Indian Removal Act of 1830. As an Indian princess, the "Chickataw" bride represented the achievement of dreams impossible in the Old World—a movement across class lines into the aristocracy and a merger with the most authentic, and yet the most reassuringly blue-eyed and European, that the New World could offer.

Anson's account is a symbolic narrative of his great-grandfather Goetsch's immigrant past that ties the family to popular stories of romantic entanglements and popular notions of encounters between Europeans and Native Americans. The story bears little or no relation to real-life experience. Still, stories like this, of migration or immigration, are a connecting thread through the diversity of American cultural groups and families. Such stories are ubiquitous, although many appear only as bare-boned accounts of their origins (the family "sailed from Breslau"), their reasons ("to get away from the high taxes"), or their route ("they traveled on the Erie Canal").

A Minnesota farmer recalled a cautionary tale about a woman who, joining her husband in Iowa, "danced across the ocean" on board ship and then had trouble negotiating the muddy, rural roads to her new home in her high heels. Other immigrant stories are rich in detail and analysis, describing the family's situation in the Old World, their motivations for leaving, their journey and dramatic incidents en route, their shock at new customs or primitive conditions, and the difficulties they overcame adjusting to a new home.

Stories of immigration legitimize family claims both to ethnic heritage and to an American identity. For example, sometime during the Napoleonic wars, Lester Buelke's great-grandfather, a twelve-year-old peasant boy, caught the eye of a Prussian officer as the boy gawked at the passing cavalry. The officer kidnapped the child, got him drunk when he cried for home, and put him into uniform. After twenty

Dorothy and Anson Goetsch driving mules, 1981. WHi(X3)38746

years of forced service, he escaped and made his way to Wisconsin. In the story, the grandfather rejected militarism and authority and risked all to secure his freedom, thus forging his family's claim to an American identity. As Anson Goetsch said, these stories help us "find out where we all fit."

Social historians study family stories as well as written documents and photographs to learn about family life in the past. Yet stories handed on from one generation to the next are often colored by hindsight, recent events, and the efforts of generations of storytellers to dramatize the past. While the family's efforts to rework or rescript the past may throw into question the historical accuracy of family stories, these developments can reveal a great deal about the family's understanding of who they are and "how they fit."[2] The different versions of events in the Krueger family's past, either written down over time or retold, reflect the ways in which they have used their own history, traditions, and ethnicity as strategic resources to meet contemporary needs for identity and cohesion. The Kruegers' finely tuned sense of who they were—presented in photographs, stories, and everyday life—has also been a source of status among their neighbors and kin.

William Krueger's Life Journey

The earliest recorded version of the Kruegers' immigrant story is a written memoir of William Krueger's life "Written by himself, with the aid of his oldest son, August, and compiled by Prof. Henry Krueger, his youngest son, May 25, 1908"—that is, at the time of William's death. The Krueger story is rich in detail and analysis. It describes the family's situation in the Old World, their motivations for leaving, their journey and dramatic incidents en route, their shock at new customs, and the difficulties they overcame adjusting to a new home:

They were twenty-eight days on the ocean, and after a good deal of sickness, they landed in New York City, April 12, 1851. They then took the boat from New York to Albany, and from Albany to Buffalo they traveled by train. From Buffalo to Milwaukee they traveled by boat. He arrived, with his family, at Milwaukee on the evening of May 13, 1851. Not wanting to spend any money to go to a hotel to stay overnight, they slept outside in a sheltered place behind some cord wood. Early the following morning two sharpers came and demanded money for staying overnight there. Not knowing the ways of the new world, he paid them what they demanded.

Tricked by con men and penniless, William walked the forty miles to his uncle's home near Lebanon.

The typescript account records the events and details of daily life. At the same time, it implies that William Krueger, through his handicraft skills, made an important contribution among the early settlers in the area:

Mr. Krueger made the wagons for the community for miles around. He received $14.00 for a complete wagon. After he had supplied all the farmers with wagons, [then] he turned his attention to the making of pumps. He also made the first wooden suction pump in [the] town of Lebanon. He received $16.00 for a pump, 30 feet long. He also made a threshing machine ... [that] could thresh from fifty to seventy bushels of wheat in a day.

"He was one of those men who are the backbone of our country"—a portentous statement that merges his immigrant, frontier farming story with a wider American identity.

The immigrant generation represented the ties and common history that bound together an increasingly far-flung, extended family. William Krueger and his third wife, Johanna, were photographed by Alex Krueger. WHi(K91)52 (left) and WHi(K91)51

In "The Life Journey of William Krueger," August and Henry assessed the meaning of William's life. They praised his many qualities: "modest, trustful," William was "of a retiring nature"; he was "a kind and loving husband and father ... one of the truest of gentlemen."

Although August took over the family farm and maintained close and friendly contacts with his conservative Baptist siblings nearby, he seems to have had more in common philosophically with his youngest brother Henry, a Milwaukee public school principal, Unitarian, and Mason. As they describe William's "Life Journey," August and Henry sound

certain themes that were important in their own understanding of how they fit. In their hands, his life story represented a movement away from intellectual, moral, and economic constraints towards greater freedom and opportunity.

Immigration represented severing ties to an old way of life and seizing new opportunities. August and Henry describe William's decision to move on: "He followed this trade in Germany until the spirit of freedom entered the hearts of young men in Germany in 1848, when he longed to come to America." The relationship between the authors' scripting of the family past and their own historical consciousness and world-view is apparent. Although there is no evidence of a relationship between William, the *Plattdeutsch*-speaking, Pomeranian immigrant farmer and the liberal German free-thinkers who immigrated to the Watertown area in 1848, August and Henry explicitly connected William's outlook to that of the urban store-keepers, professionals, and intellectuals rather than to the Old Lutheran migration and subsequent migration of land-hungry farmer-laborers, craftsmen, and servants.

There is continuity between Henry and August's version of the immigrant story: a radical break with the past, and their own break with the family's religious affiliations and their rejection of other tradition-oriented practices. August refused to join his parents' church, maintaining that religion was a matter of personal conscience; Henry joined a Unitarian church in Milwaukee. They viewed William's conversion by a German-born missionary working among Wisconsin immigrants as evidence of his independence in thought and action.

Sarah Krueger posed in her great-grandmother's skirt for a "dress-up" picture. The stool, which Edgar recalled came from his Wendorf grandparents, shows up as a prop in many family photographs. WHi(X3)37799

At about the same time that Henry and August wrote William's life story, Alex—using the family's accumulation of handmade artifacts, farm implements, and old clothing for props and William's life story as a script—recreated the immigrant experience for his camera. Soon, his cousin Willie Buelke had also posed his wife and mother with spinning wheels and other handicraft props. They wore awkward-fitting, old-time clothes, combined from different time periods and styles, buttoned somewhat haphazardly. Alex elaborated on the theme in several more photographs, with his father, children, wife, sister, and cousins dressed in the remnants of his grandparents' clothing. "Tilly Faulkman and Sarah Krueger dressed in old costumes and spinning," is set against the ax-hewn timber beams of the barn interior. The *Fachwerk* or brick-and-timber lower level of the barn was a backdrop for another photograph in which Jennie Krueger posed with many of the same props. In yet another image, Sarah Krueger, wearing the skirt that Tilly wore in the earlier photograph, and with her long hair in braids, is knitting while seated on the front porch of the old *Fachwerk* farmhouse. Alone, these immigrant dress-up photographs emphasize a static ethnicity rather than the dramatic processes of migration and Americanization. However, set in the midst of photograph albums portraying the "up and coming" Krueger family and their belongings, the visual narrative also portrays a dramatic leap from the Old World to the modern world.

More recent family history raconteurs have likely been influenced by the written memoir and the intriguing photographs. However, the Krueger family's history varies in interesting details from one storyteller to the next. Anson suggested one source of differences when he distinguished between family storytellers and family historians: "He [August Krueger] told all these things that actually happened, you know. But my uncle Bill Goetsch, he ... could make them up so that they came out real good." Both Edgar Krueger and his father's cousin, Selma Krueger Abel, recalled slightly different immigrant stories that they had learned growing up.

Edgar Krueger seemed to be Anson Goetsch's counterpart. Though he was not a storyteller by nature, Edgar was the recognized source of "reliable" family history data, and "a genius for this ancestry business" who knew "every family tree and everywhere that they lived ... way back four generations."

Edgar's cousin Lester remarked, "If you want to know something you should go down to check with Edgar. He's the family historian now." Edgar Krueger's authority rested on his fourth-generation tenure on the family farm with its storehouse of family papers. Edgar also remembered generations of the family as they talked about the past: "My grandfather would tell me quite a bit; he would recollect ... about how and what they did those days and how they did it. My dad did too ... usually as they worked." August told Edgar about life in Europe and of the auction before

the Kruegers left Rutzenhagen, Pomerania, in 1851: "A little dog they had, he said, and a stove pipe hat." Robert Krueger, when asked how his father became interested in family history, replied: "He grew up with it. He must have always been interested. We've heard about this five generations and heritage as long as I can remember."

Like his grandfather and uncle, Edgar cited economic pressure and William's opposition to "German militarism" or forced conscription as reasons for emigrating.

Edgar added details of their travels to the written account; they sailed from Hamburg to New York City and made their way to Milwaukee by way of trains, the Erie Canal, and the Great Lakes. He tells the same story of the green newcomers asked by "a couple sharpies" to pay in order to sleep beside a woodpile: "And they paid!" The next day, he said, "My great-grandfather walked out here from Milwaukee to Lebanon to that uncle. And then they came back on horses."

Prompted by a fascination with both vanishing craft skills and family history, Alex Krueger photographed his grandfather in 1899 weaving willow baskets similar to those made by day laborers in Pomerania who were too old for fieldwork. William adapted the basic North European rib-type construction used for harvesting vegetables in order to make large oval laundry baskets and egg and toy baskets. He later used just such a laundry basket as a prop in photographs sentimentalizing childhood. In another family photograph, Willie Buelke's grandmother is dressed in Old World garb as if for an immigrant tableau. The older generation, in one photograph after another, are portrayed with their handicrafts, with the Bible as evidence of their religious faith, or with newspapers respresenting their literate interest in the world around them. WHi(K91)174 (left) and WHi(B9)248

106

Edgar also described William's encounter with the uncle who had promised the newcomers assistance:

He [William Krueger's uncle] wrote such glowing reports about how nice it was in this country that they came here. When they got here, they were kind of surprised. It looked pretty primitive along here. They said he was so poor looking, 'he had a coat on that had so many holes in it nine cats couldn't catch one mouse in it!'

This remark, Edgar recalled, was always made in German, as if to convey the initial shock felt by William, who did not yet understand English.

Selma told a factually similar story of the family migration; however, her account is imbued with the drama of suffering and salvation. It is family history with a different slant. Selma agreed that her grandparents left Pomerania for economic reasons: "He could earn only $14 a year, the highest pay for wagon makers in Germany."

My grandfather [she recalled] came with a stagecoach to a certain part of Pomerania.... On the way—they had a baby girl of several weeks old—in this rough travel, rough

roads, no pavement, she died...."

Neither Edgar nor his grandfather mentioned the daughter, Bertha Adelgunda, who died en route to Wisconsin. Upon their arrival, Selma explained:

They went to Milwaukee then ... and grandpa decided [Lebanon] would be too far. The money was scarce and they did not have money to eat, so, he said, 'You stay here by this sand or stone pile—you and the children, you stay here tonight around the stone pile and sleep here if you can and I will leave some food for you so you won't get too hungry. While you sleep, I will walk to Watertown, to my friend,' which is about forty-five miles. The next day, he came back, got my grandmother and the children and they all settled in Watertown.

Selma's immigrant grandfather set right to work:

When he didn't know what else to do he made a suction

Alex photographed various signs of the world of pioneer immigrant farmers passing from the scene. In one view, Alex sits on a split-rail fence which was cut-off to make way for a newly-graded roadway. In another, he posed his parents "cradling and raking grain." WHi(K91)77 (left) and WHi(K91)410

These three photographs illustrate how amateur photographers may have prompted each other to take up a genre. Kate Renk's postcard (above) was probably the impetus for the immigrant dress-up theme which both Alex Krueger and Willie Buelke whole-heartedly embraced. Willie's version of such a photo appears top left. The Krueger family made several series on different occasions, including the photograph of "Mrs. and Mr. Alex Krueger in old German costume in barn." WHi(B91)29 (top left), WHi(K91)407 (bottom), and WHi(X3)38731

[water] pump and then a threshing machine. All in the brains of my grandfather. I think that's wonderful!

The threshing machine, which used horse- or ox-power to produce fifty to seventy-five bushels of grain in a day, found a ready market among William's neighbors. Selma, like August and Edgar, believed that William's skills gave him local prominence and made their achievement of economic goals a reality.

The different versions of the Kruegers' immigrant experience correspond to differences in attitude and belief within the Krueger family. In turn, these accounts have likely reinforced certain attitudes, including, for generations of the family, the mastery of skills, and the willingness to embrace modernization and change. Selma's parents had remained active members of the Baptist church, strictly adhering to prohibitions against smoking, dancing, card playing, drinking, and watching movies. Selma had married a Baptist minister and moved from one parish to another until she and her husband retired to Watertown. Her stories, in contrast to those of the Kruegers who remained on the farm, emphasized personal sorrows and a strong faith rather than radical departures from the past.

August's son Alex shared his progressive outlook and agrarian activist political leanings. Like his father, Alex rejected the Baptist church, not for the more established and German-identified Lutherans, but for the Congregational church in Watertown. Alex's son Edgar, a life-long Democrat in a Republican neighborhood, admired Franklin D. Roosevelt and later the civil rights movement. William's rejection of "militarism" may well have reflected and reaffirmed Edgar's opposition to the Vietnam war, an issue that divided his Watertown church.[3] Edgar's rendition of the immigrant story, and his remark that his grandfather August "looked like a typical German but he didn't think like one" are characteristic of the Krueger patriline's family stories, which celebrate a rejection of tradition in favor of "up and coming" ideas. The family stories of the immigrant generation leaving behind familiar places and family in order to make their way in America fostered an ideal of breaking new ground, of linking change with success.

The reiteration of immigrant stories like this one, generations after the event, testify to the symbolic importance of separation and renewal as an American experience. Sociologists George and Louise Spindler write that ethnicity is a sub-theme in a "fully melted" American identity. Clearly, the Kruegers' story of immigration, adjustment, and success legitimized the family's identification with widely shared American values and experiences. The circumstances surrounding characters in family stories often reveal a family's sense of place in society and history. The Kruegers' recollection of a relative who saw Lincoln and "almost spoke to him" makes the family feel closer to events in their nation's history, as does their memory of August's eagerness at age fifteen to fight in the Civil War. Edgar was quick to point out that his family's concern was not limited to their local or Pomeranian heritage:

Alex, my father, was interested in American history as a whole. It was important, always, for the family to go to the park for the Fourth of July. They taught patriotism to us children. My father and grandfather taught American values.[4]

Family Stories and Collective Memory

Stories of immigration are part of larger family repertoires that might include Dad and Mom's first date, the day the barn burned, the first car, and the time the pet gopher dug up the apple orchard. Winnie Krueger remembered hiding her bare feet the first time she met her neighbor's citified cousin Rexford Krueger, whom she later married. Everyone recalls the family joke about Tom Thomas' proposal to Mandy Goetsch: Tom calls Mandy on the telephone and blurts out, "Hello, will you marry

me?" To which Mandy replies, "Yes! Who is this?" The story of Lorena and Herbert Evans's first encounter is so familiar to family members that it has acquired a title: "Heaven Through a Screen Door."

Births and deaths, like weddings, are occasions for both family photographs and family stories; but stories tell us more about the actual event and how

Family stories are embodied in the material culture of everyday life. The tintype portrait of the youthful August Krueger and his fellow sailors, was taken in St. Joseph, Michigan, in the late 1860s and adds veracity to his stories of fishing and shipwrecks on the Great Lakes. August appears with his hat on and a cigar in his mouth. His future brother-in-law, Charles Goetsch, is there, too. Later in life, he made the detailed model of his Lake Michigan fishing boat, "Sea Gull," which his grandson then sailed on the local quarry pond. Such objects with their personal associations stand in stark contrast to the anonymity and standardization of the mass-produced consumer goods the Kruegers eagerly acquired. WHi(X2)20457 (top left), WHi(K91)267 (bottom), and WHi (K91)6

people felt. Ninety-six-year-old Lorena Evans—gently prompted by her daughter, who begins "When you were born, your mother was all alone"—plunges into a familiar story:

All alone, she cut and tied the umbilical cord and here I am. You see, she knew she was going to have a baby, so Dad had to walk nearly two miles to get the midwife. But, when he got there, she insisted—he walked so far—to have a cup of coffee before they started out again. So they had a cup of coffee and when they got back Ma had me already and she wrapped me in her petticoat.

Profound emotions of loss, death, anger, and bitterness are expressed in stories rather than in the trite photographs or funeral bouquets. Selma Abel recalled the mundane circumstances of her husband's death—"I was busy preparing dinner"—and her shock when the doctor came:

He looked at me and he said, 'He's dead.' Naturally, I started crying and he looked at me again and he said, 'You're a Christian, aren't you?' I never knew and still don't know that a Christian cannot cry when her husband dies!

Funeral photographs simply mark another milepost in the family life cycle, while Selma's grief and her resentment of the doctor's presumption are palpable in the story.

Photographs, like one of Albert A. Goetsch clowning as a beggar following a brother dressed as a banker, may joke about identity and relationships; stories flesh out the allusions. In stories of farm accidents and unlucky choices, Anson bitterly recalls his father's failed aspiration to succeed as a progressive farmer. At the same time, Anson regrets that he did not realize his dream of escaping the demands of family for a life as a cowboy. During the Great Depression, Anson moved out to Montana, worked on a ranch, and rode in the rodeos until he broke his hip:

I didn't ride anymore ... so I came back home and was cornered. My mother and my brother younger than me just had a row. He was moving off and she owned all the cattle and stuff and nobody to tend it.... I got tangled in that and that's how I happened to stay here 'cause otherwise my heart was really set out there in Montana.

Stories of farm accidents—a hand crushed by the windmill or a disabling fall that ends with a family struggling to survive—also remind listeners of their dependence on one another. Family tension surfaced in often repeated statements, half joke and half warning, like Ernie Buelke's comment—repeated by his nephew—that, if Lester did anything on the farm, his father Willie would always say, "We did it," and if they did it together, Willie would always say, "I did it."

Other stories celebrate lucky escapes. August Krueger—a young man "so strong he could lift the front end of a horse off the ground on his shoulders"—set off to work on a Lake Michigan fishing boat. He later captained a boat out of St. Joseph, Michigan, that was wrecked in a storm. Edgar's version of this event concludes with the cryptic remark, in German, "the sea has no timbers." August returned home—to a family world that had, literally, the security of timbers—to take over and continue the family's successful farming enterprise. In achievement or failure, these often repeated stories locate the individual and the family in relationship to events, explaining where they are and how they got there.

Stories of family visits often remind us that

different people have different ways. Bertha Goetsch was a family heroine who managed to feed and care for seven children. By contrast, on a visit to Iowa, her mother-in-law, Charlotte Goetsch, was the domineering, "full-blooded German" grandmother. Lorena described the visit:

That was Charlotte.... Oh my, how we hated her. [She and her husband] came out and stayed all summer with his [William's] two sisters and brothers.... The two sisters, they liked to keep him, grandfather, but they didn't want her! My mother had to keep Grandma and I didn't dare to play or nothing. 'You get in the house,' in German she said it. 'Wash those dishes, you've got fine fingers for that!' When Ma would give us a piece of bread [she would say] 'Bertha, Bertha, them kids eat too much. How can you afford it? You can't afford it.' Ma said, 'They're going to have something to eat when they're hungry if it's the last piece of bread I've got!' That's talking up to your mother-[in-law]!

Memorable relatives, like Bertha and Charlotte, became stock characters in stories the Kruegers told to dramatize the family's past.

Storytelling, as Edgar suggested, often accompanied mundane chores and, perhaps as a result, women told somewhat different stories than their husbands or male cousins. While women were often, as social historian George Lipsitz has suggested, "relegated to the margins" of men's stories, women were far more often at the center of the stories women told. Their stories emphasized heroism in the day-to-day struggle to provide for a family. Women also

Photographs evoke stories and even memories of picture-making events. Sweethearts Rose and Ernie Buelke strike a pose for Willie's camera; Alex Goetsch, Herbert Evans, William Goetsch, and Lorena Evans play at "pouring a libation," while out on a picnic. The practice of concocting visual photographic jokes was carried over from the earlier glass-plate negatives to this later view (right) on roll film. WHi(B91)175 (left) and WHi(X3)37784

112

passed on accounts of particular significance to other women, from stories of sexual exploitation to accounts of childbirth. Often these stories reaffirmed that generations of women had helped each other in crisis, and in ways that sometimes ran counter to family or public expectations.

Krueger family stories encompass over a century of experience in Wisconsin; yet their stories of the immigrant experiences have held a particular fascination for subsequent generations. The Kruegers have frequently shared, revised, and added to their family repertoire, which begins with accounts of William and Wilhelmina's departure for Wisconsin. These collective memories reinforce the sense of family identity that has engendered mutual assistance, contacts over long distances, and access to wider spheres of experience and enterprise. As a result, the world in which the Kruegers strive, succeed, and find recognition is, to some extent, the product of their storytelling and family myth-making activities. However, these idealized and sentimental associations with a pioneer immigrant past, which were a source of cohesion and advancement, have also led, in recent times, to both bitterness between close kin and restricted opportunities.

Successive generations tailor their memories, add new stories, and pass them on to be cut apart and sewn up in a new style by the next generation. Each family member shapes a unique rendition of the family history from a repertoire constituted in the past and continually enriched by new experiences and events. While family members may remember it differently, their history has a common character; though they frequently select different memories, they recognize the fundamental importance of the

"We were playing Jew," Lester Buelke later recalled, which was not surprising since the few Jewish families in rural Wisconsin communities were sometimes rag and scrap dealers. WHi(B91)91

family past. From this perspective, there seems to be a collective, unified vision of the Krueger family.

Through written histories, personal narratives, photograph albums, and the repetition and re-examination of stories, the Kruegers and their kin have reflected upon and structured the past to fit the emotional needs and concerns of the present. Just as families experience the consequences of events together, they select, organize, and explain their past together as a group, all the while adjusting the past to fit new circumstances and needs. A shared family identity defines and gives significance to what a family does, has done, and will do. The act of remembering, itself, becomes a ritual of family ties and continuity.

Landscapes of Farm Family Life

When August "commenst farming" for himself, his ledger showed wheat as the major cash crop, supplemented by oats, barley, hay, potatoes, and rutabagas. The family also kept hogs, horses, sheep, and a few dairy cows. By the 1880s, however, August and Mary Krueger had established dairy farming as the basis of their livelihood. Dairying involved a new family work routine, dictated by the daily demands of producing milk, in contrast to the seasonal demands of raising grain. Milk, in turn, required speedy transport and processing—initially into cheese—which enmeshed farmers in a world of schedules, cooperatives, marketing, and transportation.

Material changes came both with shifts in the economic basis of family farming and the development of new technology. A reaper and later a binder replaced the cradle scythes that men swung to cut the wheat and the rakes women used to make sheaves bound with straw. The reaper had long sweeps that placed the grain on a platform in bunches; a man standing in the rear would work "hard and fast" to tie the bunches into bundles. The binder did the job of tying the bundles as well.

The products of modern technology did not automatically sweep the American countryside; people had to learn about them and decide to use them; they had to be convinced. Local storekeepers and implement salesmen urged them to buy. Newspaper advertisements, magazine articles, and equipment displays at fairs carried a twin message: "machines will make things easier" and "machines will make you a success." The university's "short courses" taught farmers and their sons how to choose crops and machines, how to manage work, and, above all, how to make changes in the name of "scientific farming." Younger family members seized these opportunities; Alex Krueger took the dairy short course less than a decade after it was established. His cousin recalled, "They did things just as modern as they could." Alex introduced alfalfa, a higher-quality cattle feed, replaced the Red Durham dairy herd with Holsteins, and acquired a tractor, a binder, a seed drill, and a hay-loader. "Then," Edgar said, "we didn't have it so hard."

Alex Krueger and Willie Buelke, the family's farmer-photographers, demonstrated a dynamic sense of how the past had forged the familiar landscape and of how new technologies had encroached

Over many years, Willie Buelke gathered material evidence of the dramatic changes he had see in farm technology and everyday life. This "museum" of technological history filled several sheds and included a jumble of yokes, a rocking horse and other toys, farm implements along with his collection of deteriorating glass plate negatives stored above his garage. Photographed by David Mandel in 1979. WHi Lot 4303

upon that landscape. It is not so surprising that Willie Buelke later filled several sheds with a collection of old-time artifacts and new tools testifying to the physical transformation of his world. As the poet Archibald MacLeish said, the past is embedded in the landscapes of rural America:

We tell our freedom backward by the land

We tell our past by the gravestones and the apple trees.[1]

Fascinated with the transformation of the artifacts, buildings, and agricultural landscapes from the backwoods, of the immigrant enclave to the modern, commercialized, scientific enterprise, Alex repeatedly photographed the farm profile outlined against the horizon. Photography produced a tangible expression of place and heightened the family's profound, collective awareness of it.

Their image of the farm, the buildings, and the land were fused with the Kruegers' collective identity. The material changes in farming and in the setting of family life came as the Krueger family responded to the market economy, to mass culture, and new consumer patterns. The physical setting, built and transformed over time, embodied ideas beyond everyday use. The interaction of experience, memory, and perceptions of place carried over into the home; as the Kruegers made, bought, and kept

things, artifacts, too, served as a reservoir for a complex sense of who they were and how they fit in relationship to the past, to the local scene, and to larger currents in American life.

Generational continuity and the realities of modernization pushed and pulled at the Kruegers' view of their world; yet in photographs they confidently asserted that their lives and their farm were, in a tangible, material sense, of their own making. This chapter explores the convergence of landscapes and events and the role of hand-crafted, mass-manufactured, and simply old belongings in the dynamics of everyday family life and family identity.

Making Things

William Krueger, the wagonmaker, belonged to the first generation of Pomeranian farm laborers' sons who were free to choose their occupation. Like many other tradesmen, he faced the intense competition brought on by a population boom and an over-supply

The Kruegers were very familiar with this view of their farm from the south-east fields because of long hours spent there during the seasonal farmwork of planting and harvesting crops. The farmscape, much like group portraits from reunions, called forth stories of a shared family past. Alex photographed the view in 1900 and then again in 1932 after the new dairy barn was constructed. The Krueger children became familiar with the workings of a farm from a different perspective. They played at farmwork with wooden toys like these from the model farm Alex built with his jigsaw. The barn and animals first belonged to the twins, and later were handed down to Edgar's grandchildren. WHi(K91)443 (top left), WHi(K91)667 (bottom left), and WHi(X2)20458 (right)

William Krueger may have built the wagon in this photograph of a family gathering going for a Sunday ride in a lumber wagon, about 1908. WHi(K91)517

of skilled workers. In Wisconsin, William used his woodworking skills to build wagons and implements such as drags, hand rakes, flails, and a horse-drawn threshing machine; his skills ensured the family's survival. After his retirement, William continued to make furniture, toys, and useful gadgets. In old age, he wove the type of willow baskets used to harvest potatoes in his Pomeranian home village of Stargordt. William's son, Albert, learned woodworking skills from his father and successfully combined local carpentry work with farming. However, the adoption of frame construction, as in the house Albert and August built for the newlyweds Alex and Flora, represented the assimilation of changing patterns of everyday life.[2]

In the next generation, family account books and ledgers revealed a steady need for minor repairs on farm machinery. Bailing wire and ingenuity might do for some jobs, but a blacksmith was needed for the hard ones. It took time and money to take an implement to a blacksmith's shop to get it fixed. When small, portable forges became available, the University of Wisconsin's College of Agriculture offered a course in blacksmithing for farm repairs. Alex Krueger took the course in 1896, adding a new skill to the ones he had learned from his family. As mass production developed, however, the value of these skills diminished in the marketplace and they became less necessary at home.

Competition from mass-produced goods changed the role of craft skills on the farm from economic necessity to useful supplement, and then to mere recreation. Like William, Albert and August carved wooden models and made toys for their children and grandchildren. Alex purchased woodworking equipment and made jigsaw-cut toy figures and spindle-turned toys for the little ones. To Alex, the grandparents' craft skills, like the local *Fachwerk* houses and split-rail fences, represented vanishing peasant ways, witness both to the transformation in everyday life wrought by new technology and to his own family's success.

The Krueger women also shared a tradition of craft skills, although fewer examples of their needlework, quilting, crocheting, and knitting survived everyday use. Sarah Krueger is remembered as an excellent seamstress who made clothing for herself, her mother, sister-in-law, nephew, and niece. In photographs, the children's elaborate lace collars, stylish doll clothing, miniature quilts, stuffed animals, and dolls testify to the craft output of women, now largely worn out or used up. That Shirley, Bea, and

Selma, Albert Krueger's daughter, with her grandfather's hand-carved figures and a toy baby buggy filled with store-bought dolls. WHi(K91)99

other women have lovingly maintained examples of needlework, crochet, and quilts—now folded away in dresser drawers in a back bedroom—reflects the more subtle strand of women's family history-making activities. The carefully maintained but hidden textiles are a tangible metaphor of the less public transmission of women's folklore in the family.

Buying Things

The Kruegers and their kin, in households across the Midwest, have "cobbled together" family and individual identity from a mix of consumer goods and memorabilia. In the years following Alex and Flora's marriage, the farm family celebrated their

sense of having achieved the goals of immigration and of becoming a successful and Americanized family. While images, stories, and artifacts reflect both ethnic identification and a concern for their own family and rural past, the Kruegers were also very much in touch with the popular culture of the early twentieth century. Alex and Flora Krueger made purchases from department stores and took

pride after their wedding, in their new china, and later in their new Chevrolet. They were proud, too, of the new appliances—the radio, a mixer, a new kitchen range—which they purchased after electrical lines reached the farmhouse.

Investment, innovation, and equipment were essential to "progressive" agriculture; however, with typical Germanic caution, the Kruegers avoided going into debt to buy machinery, land, or new appliances. Anson Goetsch explained:

The Kruegers? They were much slower at buying stuff. Like I said, they wanted to see that they had the money before they went and bought it.... Then what helped them was that it was from father to son, you know.

From mixers to milking equipment, farm family life was about change as well as continuity. After they brought electric lines up to the house in 1936, Alex documented the newly acquired appliances: Flora displays the oven, a refrigerator, a radio, and a Hamilton Beach mixer. Edgar later took a snapshot of his wife with their daughter and daughter-in-law in the remodeled kitchen. In order to up-date to the look of a modern suburban ranch home, they replaced heavy farmhouse wooden moldings around the windows and doors with narrower, painted trim. Below, left, the double barn doors stand open to frame a view of the neighboring Scholz farm. WHi(X2)20461 (top left), WHi(X3)38115, and WHi(X3)38069 (right)

About 1910, the Albert A. Goetsch family pose with his first car, a Studebaker EMF or, as it was later remembered, "Every Morning Fix." As the automobile grills became more elaborate, family photographers shifted away from the typical side view (formerly used for photographing horse-drawn wagons) in order to feature the chrome-grated front-end. Here Bob Krueger stands proudly next to his slightly dented Chevy. WHi(K93)7 (left) and WHi(K91)529

Although he was excited by new methods and increasing expectations, Alex Krueger sufficiently mistrusted the agricultural markets and business sectors that he was moved to join the radical, farm activist, Non-Partisan League—an extremely unusual move for a Wisconsin dairy farmer.[3] Yet the move reflected the tradition of progressive "free-thinker" attitudes attributed to William and the independent, populist politics identified with August.

Jennie Krueger on the porch of the Fachwerk *farmhouse with her dolls. Her aunt Sarah sewed and crocheted Jennie's dress as well as the doll dresses and cradle quilt. WHi(K91)275*

122

For all the short courses and salesmen's pitches, innovations sometimes did not work. A wrong decision could ruin a farmer as fast as a depression, as Alex's uncle, Albert Goetsch learned:

He was advanced more than any of the neighbors around there. He had the first car in the neighborhood and the first tractor which he would have been better off if he never had. There were threshing machines around but they were all pulled by steam engines. But my Dad, he bought one of the first [gasoline driven] tractors that come out.... That's really what broke my Dad. The motor went to pieces three or four times. He had it bought and signed a note for it and he still had to pay for it.

Although Albert had attended the University of Wisconsin short course and "was always quite high up" on innovative farming, his innovations, from tractors to registered Holstein cows, Duroc hogs, and Percheron horses also produced a relentless crop of problems. His farming enterprise rarely lived up to the neatly printed cards which advertised "A.A. Goetsch, Pine Grove Stock Farm." In 1921, at age fifty-seven, Albert was kicked by a horse and died. Settling the estate in hard times left his widow Tillie only forty acres; her seven children helped her work the farm and buy back the land.

Decisions about costly improvements sometimes burdened family relations as well as family finances. Albert Goetsch's son recalled his parents' lengthy arguments about farm decisions which involved capital she brought to farm operation with their marriage. Edgar and Alex disagreed sharply over shifting to grade-A (fresh) milk production; Alex saw too much risk in new equipment and government inspections. Edgar made the switch in 1946, after decades of disagreement.

Keeping Things

In a photograph captioned "Mr. And Mrs. Wm. Krueger spinning and making baskets. 1900," Alex recorded his grandfather and step-grandmother seated on a split-log bench beside their log house, practicing vanishing, traditional craft skills: spinning and basket-making. Alex photographed other "survivals" of old-time and ethnic ways, including *Fachwerk* houses and barns and split-rail fences. Photographs of family elders staged with props representing the past are a ubiquitous part of the Kruegers' photographic collections, as they are in many another midwestern family.

As much as immigrant stories, these hand-made objects, skills, and photographs represent for the Kruegers the experience of the immigrant generation achieving in America the prosperity and security they had sought. For the Kruegers, as for other immigrants, success meant amassing property that could be passed on to their children. Just as farm land formed an important legacy, so did the accumulation of store-bought and hand-made objects, documents, correspondence, journals, and memorabilia that each generation handed down.

In a study of a New Englander with a similar role as family curator, historian Grant McCracken described the old farmhouse, in the family for seven generations, and its contents as "a center for the family, a proof of its longevity, a container of its memories." McCracken found that the past swamped and tyrannized contemporary life in a way that many would find intolerable.[4] The Kruegers, like many other families, have responded more flexibly over time, recasting symbolic artifacts and

123

rescripting the past to fit present circumstances.

The Krueger photographs reveal ways new media reinforced existing family patterns while creating new modes of expression adapted to changing times and circumstances. Photographic tableaux displaying baskets, hand-carved toys, spinning wheels, and other "ethnic" or "immigrant" artifacts seem to have been their way of refining and personalizing an increasingly mass-produced environment. Yet the family's assimilation from traditional or immigrant peasant patterns to modern consumer patterns was neither sudden nor complete. William and Wilhelmina Krueger broke with traditional patterns when they emigrated, and the family subsequently took pride in success achieved through that dramatic departure. Following emigration, the Kruegers, like other immigrant families, gradually adopted modern patterns in certain areas of their family lives while adapting or retaining traditional patterns in others. The first generation used traditional skills and methods in shaping their farm life in Wisconsin within the limitations of the new setting; the second generation maintained, often unself-consciously, many of these traditional ways—making use in particular of carpentry skills—while rejecting others.[5] The third generation continued some traditional patterns, rejected others, and began to memorialize and sentimentalize still others. Family life was thus a blend of mainstream and ethnic, mass-produced and hand-made, urban and rural.

These photographs were obviously taken to record newly acquired goods. Willie Buelke's children and their cousins pose outside a Juneau, Wisconsin, home, amidst a conspicuous display of elaborate playthings. The Krueger twins proudly display the brand-new Edison phonograph and wax cylinders. Jennie is holding Tramp, who posed patiently in various doll dresses. WHi(B91)30 (top) and WHi(K91)356

Like other middle-class Americans at the turn of the century, the Kruegers freighted commonplace artifacts of everyday life with meaning. Moved by the personal associations embodied in objects and surroundings, family members who had moved away from the farm, like Henry Krueger, maintained ties to the rural life that represented unaffected sincerity, the tangible satisfactions of productive labor, and an escape from the frenetic and degrading attributes of urban and public life.[6] Even as the preponderance of Americans came to live in cities in the early twentieth century, popular literature and illustrations associated the farm home with love, nurturing, honesty, permanence, and bounty.

The products of handcraft processes contrasted with the "up and coming" world of manufactured goods. At the turn of the century, the Kruegers' celebration of themselves drew upon both these nostalgic images, their participation in mainstream culture represented by leisure pursuits, enthusiastic purchases, and displays of mass-produced goods. For Alex and Flora Krueger, there was no lag between popular consumption patterns and their own activities.

The interaction between the Kruegers' perceptions of farm family life and the decisions that they made regarding the farm spiraled in the twentieth century. The familiar setting, infused with sentiment, bound the family together but also became a hindrance to transmitting valuable property from one generation to the next. Although married and moved off the farm, Jennie Krueger's economic interests in the property were compounded by her nostalgic attachment to the "home place" as represented in idyllic childhood imagery. Jennie, according to her

nephew Bob, believed she would not feel "at home" there if her parents sold the farm to Edgar. Alex and Flora, encouraged by Jennie, were not eager to sell out and either assume a secondary position on the farm as William had done or retire to town like August and Mary. While Alex had actively explored the possibilities of buying land as far away as Alabama, Edgar and Elna, confronting both the economic constraints of the Depression and the prospect of severing connections, did not consider moving beyond the immediate area.

At the turn of the century, Alex Krueger and his family selected objects that articulated or affirmed their vision of the family past. New media, like photography, reinforced family patterns while creating new channels adapted to changing times and circumstances. The continuing appearance of family memorabilia in photographs and displays over decades and generations documents their symbolic significance and, in turn, elaborates and extends the meanings conveyed by the objects. Time and use have given legitimacy to stories and ideas linked with the objects that the Kruegers cherish and display in the present. For example, in a 1950s snapshot, Jennie, dressed in a gathered, square-dancing skirt, posed with her grandmother's stool and a spinning wheel. The backdrop of a sentimental wallpaper scene depicting European peasant life reinforces the romanticization of the family's past. While Alex and Flora showcased their participation in consumer culture, these consumer artifacts have come to represent the twins' childhood, an idyllic period in the family's past.

In the homes of the following generation, the artifacts appear, refurbished, in family history

This photograph records the second generation household in 1901. August and Mary sit with their daughter Sarah at a table draped in a fringed and embroidered cloth. The windows are hung with lace curtains, and a small wall shelf—decorated with a crocheted border—fills the wall space between them, crowded with photographs and bric-a-brac. Numerous plants grow from pots on the window sills and tables, and vines creep across the windows and over a nearby cabinet. In the midst of this crowded ornamentation, each family member is seen reading, while a copy of the Watertown Weltbürger, *the local German-language newspaper, is propped prominently on the floor. The objects and newspaper give tangible evidence of each household's sense of identity. Alex made similar photographs of the two other households that shared the farm. WHi((X3)37814*

displays. In the living room of their ranch-style house, Bob Krueger laughed over a brightly colored, jigsaw-cut, wooden farm animal: "Yeah, my farm was kind of unusual. You know, I had the only farm in Wisconsin with penguins." His grandfather, Alex Krueger, had cut out, constructed, and painted the barns and sheds with their unusual livestock for his children and grandchildren. In 1980, Bob and his wife Bea spread the scale-model farm beneath their Christmas tree. They trimmed the fresh-cut spruce with a mix of new and old family ornaments including delicate, painted glass tear-drops that may have hung on strings from the ceiling of a Watertown department store eighty or ninety years earlier. The family's Christmas display reaches back as far; in 1905, when Bob's father and aunt, Edgar

and Jennie were children, they posed for a Christmas postcard with the same model farm. Objects from the shared past voice associations with family memories, a nostalgia for a rural way of life, and a comforting sense of familiarity and continuity.

However, the meaning of the family history, condensed in symbolic objects, photographs, documents, and stories, has changed dramatically over the past century. For Bob and Shirley, the family farm and history conveyed bittersweet associations that belied the professed comfort and happiness of family life in the previous generations. Although they left farming, both Bob and Shirley married and remained in the Watertown area enmeshed in webs of kinship, social ties, and history. Bob's break with family farming resulted in a sense of loss rather than a sense of continuity with the family's stories of dramatic departures and new directions. As a result, they have revised the history script, centered on a nostalgic, static rendition of the past, represented in family artifacts, as a comfort in the face of transitions that include the deaths of their parents Edgar and Elna Krueger and the sale of the family's century farm. The Kruegers and Oestreichs have re-scripted the family past to suppress contradictions

with their present circumstances. The Kruegers have interpreted artifacts adaptively to dramatize their common membership in both a distinctive family and in a larger ethnic-American identity.

Following his death, Edgar's children and grandchildren chafed at restrictions imposed by the auctioneer when the family belongings were sold; family members sought to purchase prized pieces of memorabilia. However, the auctioneer, concerned that these items were the most valuable and the most likely to attract competitive bids, refused to make advance sales. Edgar's children and grandchildren purchased a few items: woodworking tools, a saddle,

In 1979, Shirley displayed many of the objects from the immigrant dress-up photographs around the fireplace of the Oestreich's Watertown home. When the farm goods were later auctioned off, Shirley added her father's accordian to the collection which includes the tin lantern, the Watertown ceramic jug, and the spinning wheel. Photograph by David Mandel. WHi(X2)20460

and a few pieces of turn-of-the-century department store or mail-order furniture. Elna Krueger had not shared in the cult of Krueger family history; her collection of porcelain birds did not, in turn, attract the same attention from her children and grandchildren when the farm goods were auctioned off in 1988.

127

Sarah may have taken this picture of Mr. and Mrs. Alex Krueger fixing up the tree, on Christmas Eve, 1901.
The clutter reflected in the mirror suggests the day-to-day use of family photographs. WHi(K91)167

Conclusion

The geographer Yi-Fu Tuan asserts that, in the process of generating a sense of place in the modern world, "words and gestures are ephemeral compared with objects."[7] For the Kruegers, spinning wheels, wooden shoes, and clay pipes represent the immigrant past while gadgets like their Victrola with its polished brass horn once symbolized their "up-and-coming" interests. In later life, Alex's photographic mentor, Willie Buelke, expanded on these interests in a "museum" he assembled in sheds behind his daughter's home. There he displayed "pioneer" artifacts and the progress of technology from ox bows to Model Ts. His collection, like Alex Krueger's photographs, served not so much to preserve as to measure the past and the distance the family or rural neighborhood had traveled.

The passage up the Kruegers' farm driveway–between two massive fir trees planted over a century ago, past the sided-over *Fachwerk* house, the barns and sheds, the turn-of-the-century farmhouse and the modern garage, and the view out over open country, orderly farm land and windbreaks, the old quarry and, to the southeast, Bob and Bea

Krueger's contemporary ranch house—is a passage through family history. As Edgar walked the drive, he often pointed out the foundations of earlier half-timbered and log barns and the outlines of the former orchard and garden, now marked only by a few remaining trees. In the 1970s and 1980s, the *Fachwerk* house was occupied by a tenant family whose children grew up on the Krueger farm and regarded Edgar as a "grandpa." The old blacksmith shed contained William Krueger's workbench, his grandson Alex's forge, and Edgar's collection of license plates. In the attic of the late-nineteenth-century farmhouse where he grew up, Edgar kept spindle-turned high chairs and cribs, stacks of *National Geographic* magazines, baskets, carved wooden toys, his father's old camera, and a hodgepodge of other belongings. The interior of the house,

remodeled when Edgar and Elna bought the farm in 1957, resembled a suburban tract house. The large, well-lighted kitchen contained honey-colored oak cabinets, a Formica table, and vinyl chairs. They had replaced the original heavy, dark-stained woodwork with the narrow, lightly painted door and window frames common to suburban homes. For Edgar, the farm, embodying the multi-layered family past more than any assortment of artifacts, photographs, and documents, gave voice to the family's experiences and values.

A family's perception of its past is constructed from a clutter of stories, ideas, photographs, papers, and belongings handed on by previous generations. Objects like photographs can convey meanings for individuals and families far beyond their everyday usefulness. This is evident in the fact that conflicts may arise over the possession of treasured memorabilia that are far out of proportion to the object's real value. The Kruegers' history is marked by contradictions and painful ironies. They gave up the Pomeranian dialect and customs as old-fashioned, but they retained their pride in their immigrant origins; the numerous photographs and artifacts valued by the family as symbols of identity and unity have also been sources of family disputes.

Families weave tradition and ritual from the things that surround them—from an old lantern, a cherished embroidery, a baby's silver spoon, or a child's store-bought toy. Family photographs and family stories often focus on such homely posessions, which evoke memories of "the time when..." or of "Aunt

Alex photographed a procession of new and used cars and he hung up each old license plate on the doors of his blacksmith shop. 1979 photograph of Edgar Krueger by David Mandel. WHi(X2)20462

Sarah," memories that reaffirm the family's vision of itself and its history. The scholar can read "objective" history in a collection of artifacts, but the many small things that people remember, pass on, and invent are everyday, tangible links to the past.

William Krueger's descendants use his baskets and toys, other hand-crafted objects, and the turn-of-the-century photographs to define themselves, and, through that sense of shared identity, to maintain a sometimes supportive and sometimes hindering or over-complicated network of kin. Not all the Kruegers' efforts to sustain continuity have pro-

duced the intended results. All in all, however, the family has succeeded in converting the clutter of everyday life into an armory from which they have responded to the world around them.

Photographs—still passed around and admired in the family—give significance to surviving artifacts. In 1979, Krueger project photographer, David Mandel, found that Alex's anvil and forge, his grandfather's workbench, and the tools used by the men of the family, still stood in the shed he had used as a blacksmith shop in 1911. WHi(X2)20463 (left) and WHi(K91)513

131

Notes on Sources

THE research for this project rests on privately held documents, county records, and the considerable collections of the State Historical Society of Wisconsin. Most of the sources relating directly to the Krueger family and farm in Dodge County, Wisconsin, have been gathered together at the State Historical Society in Madison; these include microfilmed family papers such as letters, contracts, account books, memoirs, obituaries, and genealogies. Family members generously donated the original negatives produced by Alexander Krueger, William Buelke, and Rexford Krueger. Between 1976 and 1987, many family members and local people were interviewed; and those tape-recorded interviews and abstracted transcripts are also part of the Krueger Family Collections. Unpublished research reports for the collections and buildings of Old World Wisconsin provided crucial data. United States Census records contained a wealth of information; these included the annual summaries of population and agriculture as well as the federal manuscript censuses of 1860, 1870, 1880, 1900, and 1910 for Lebanon and Emmet townships, Dodge County, Wisconsin. The Wisconsin state censuses for Emmet and Lebanon townships for 1885, 1895, and 1905 provided glimpses of the Kruegers in the intervening years. Maps, city directories, local histories, college yearbooks, newspapers (among them the *Watertown Chronicle*, the *Watertown Daily Times*, and the *Watertown Gazette*) and periodicals such as the *Wisconsin Farmer* and *Hoard's Dairyman* illustrated the changing local scene.

Dodge County records at the county courthouse in Juneau provided wills and deeds as well as marriage, birth, and death records. Research at the Watertown Historical Society and the Watertown Public Library produced photographs of the local scene as well as local histories, church histories, maps, and miscellaneous collections.

The following endnotes are a guide to works that we have relied on over the course of the project. Except where quoted directly, each work is cited but once.

Willie Buelke photographed this view of a nearby dam. WHi(B91)230

Six Generations Here

1. The late architectural historian Richard W. E. Perrin and Pomeranian specialist Hans Keuther lobbied for the establishment of an outdoor museum which ultimately emerged as Old World Wisconsin. During the early 1960s Perrin published a series of articles in the *Wisconsin Magazine of History* which was reissued in book form as *The Architecture of Wisconsin* (Madison, 1967); he also wrote *Historic Wisconsin Buildings: A Survey of Pioneer Architecture, 1835-1870* (Milwaukee, 1962). My thanks to past and current staff of Old World Wisconsin–including Emilie Tari, Marty Perkins, Alan Pape, and Mark Knipping. See also Richard H. Zeitlin, *Germans in Wisconsin* (Madison, 1977).

2. This text reflects ideas about photography and autobiography developed by George A. Talbot in *At Home: Domestic Life in the Post-Centennial Era, 1876-1920* (Madison, 1977).

3. I wish to thank archivists Bonnie Wilson of the Minnesota Historical Society, and Mary Bennett of the Iowa Historical Society, author of *An Iowa Album: A Photographic History, 1860-1920* (Iowa City, 1995).

4. Yi-Fu Tuan, "Rootedness vs. Sense of Place," in *Landscape* (Winter, 1980), 24:3-8.

5. See Kenneth L. Ames, *Beyond Necessity: Art in the Folk Tradition* (Winterthur, Delaware, 1977); "Meaning in Artifacts: Hall Furnishings in Victorian America," in the *Journal of Interdisciplinary History* (Summer, 1978) 9:19-46; and *Death in the Dining Room and Other Tales of Victorian Culture* (Philadelphia, 1992). See also Daniel Rodgers, *The Work Ethic in Industrial America, 1850-1920* (Chicago, 1978).

6. Robert C. Ostergren, *A Community Transplanted: The Trans-Atlantic Experience of a Swedish Immigrant Settlement in the Upper Middle West, 1835-1915* (Madison, 1988).

7. See Kathleen Neils Conzen, *Immigrant Milwaukee, 1836-1860: Accommodation and Community in a Frontier City* (Cambridge, 1976); "The Germans," in Stephan Thernstrom, ed., *Harvard Encyclopedia of American Ethnic Groups* (Cambridge, 1980), 406-425; "Immigrants in Nineteenth-Century Agricultural History," in Lou Ferleger, ed., *Agriculture and National Development: Views on the Nineteenth Century* (Ames, Iowa, 1990), 303-342; and Kathleen Neils Conzen *et al.*, "The Invention of Ethnicity: A Perspective from the U.S.A.," in *Journal of American Ethnic History* (Fall, 1992), 12:3-41.

The Kruegers: Farm and Family

1. James J. Sheehan's encyclopedic *German History, 1770-1866* (Oxford, 1989) examines rural life in the wider context of cultural, political, and economic developments. See Mack Walker, *Germany and the Emigration, 1816-1885* (Cambridge, 1964); H. J. Habakkuk, "Family Structure and Economic Change in Nineteenth Century Europe," in *The Family*, ed. by Rose Laub Coser (New York, 1974); and LaVern J. Rippley, *The German-Americans* (Lanham, Maryland, 1984). A locally printed, 1953 pamphlet provided by Krueger relatives in Germany, *Druck George Koenig Koln, "Adrian Von Vorke, Un Leber Mit Voll Blutern,"* described the "home place" in Pomerania.

2. Liselotte Clemens, *Old Lutheran Emigration from Pomerania to the U. S. A.: History and Motivation, 1839-1843* (Hamburg, 1976).

3. See the discussion of local and community history in Thomas Bender, *Community and Social Change in America* (Baltimore, 1978). For the study of the family in history, see Martine Segalen, *Historical Anthropology of the Family* (Cambridge, 1986); William Thomas and Florian Znaniecki, *The Polish Peasant in Europe and America,* 3 vols. (Chicago, 1918-1920); Tamara K. Hareven, "The Family as Process; The Historical Study of the Family Cycle," in the *Journal of Social History,* 7:322-329 (1974) and "The History of the Family and the Complexity of Social Change," in the *American Historical Review,* 96:95-124 (February, 1991); David J. Russo, *Families and Communities: A New View of American History* (Nashville, 1974); and Rayna Rapp, Ellen Ross, and Renate Bridenthal, "Examining Family History," in *Feminist Studies,* 5:174-200 (1979).

4. Willard W. Cochrane, *The Development of American Agriculture: A Historical Analysis* (Minneapolis, 1979).

5. University of Wisconsin, *Fifty Years of Cooperative Extension in Wisconsin, 1912-1962* (Madison, 1962).

Their Stake in the Land

1. Contrary to the claim of Marcus Lee Hansen in a much-cited sentence in *The Immigrant in American History* (New York, 1964; originally published 1940), 66.

2. 1900 census figures and estimates from Joseph Och, *Der Deutschamerikanische Farmer: Sein Anteil an der Eroberung und Kolonisation der Bundesdomäne der Ver. Staaten besonders in den Nord Centralstaaten* (Columbus, Ohio, 1913), 67, 73.

3. These figures are based on self-descriptions of ancestry; they include all persons who report a given ancestry, regardless of whether it is single or multiple. "German" includes descendants of eighteenth-century German colonists, as well as those whose ancestors were part of the massive nineteenth-century immigration. Proportions calculated from U.S. Bureau of the Census, *1990 Census of Population: Social and Economic Characteristics of Wisconsin, "Ancestry, 1990,"* pp. 72, 210, 212.

4. The map is compiled from U.S. Bureau of the Census, TIGER/Line Census Files, 1990 Census of Population and Housing, Summary Tape File 3A, with the assistance of Sammaramish

Data Systems, GeoSight Face Finder. I wish to thank Christopher Winters of the Regenstein Library, University of Chicago, for his assistance with this program. For nineteenth-century patterns, see Kate Asaphine Everest, "How Wisconsin Came By Its Large German Element," in the *Wisconsin Historical Collections*, 12 (Madison, 1881-1883), 299-334.

5. U.S. Bureau of the Census, *1990 Census of Population: Social and Economic Characteristics. United States*, Table 12, "*Ancestry, 1990,*" p. 12.

6. Proportions compiled from *Table 17*, "*Ancestry, 1990,*" of the *1990 Census of Population: Social and Economic Characteristics* volumes for Illinois, Indiana, Iowa, Kansas, Michigan, Minnesota, Missouri, Nebraska, North Dakota, Ohio, South Dakota, and Wisconsin.

7. Recent scholarship includes Klaus J. Bade, ed., *Population, Labour and Migration in 19th and 20th Century Germany* (Leamington Spa, 1987); Dirk Hoerder and Jurg Nagler, eds., *People in Transit: German Migrations in Comparative Perspective, 1820-1930* (Cambridge, England, 1995); and Leslie Page Moch, *Moving Europeans: Migration in Western Europe Since 1650* (Bloomington, 1992). For the American side of this migration process, see Kathleen Neils Conzen, "A Saga of Families," in Clyde A. Milner II, Carol A. O'Connor, and Martha A. Sandweiss, eds., *The Oxford History of the American West* (New York, 1994), 315-357.

8. For German immigration to Wisconsin, consult Everest, "How Wisconsin Came By Its Large German Element"; Kate Everest Levi, "Geographical Origin of German Immigration to Wisconsin," *Wisconsin Historical Collections,* 14 (Madison, 1890); Freistadt Historical Society, *Freistadt and the Lutheran Immigration* (Mequon, Wisconsin, 1989); and Myron E. Gruenwald, *Baltic Teutons: Pioneers of America's Frontier* (Oshkosh, Wisconsin, 1988).

9. For these examples of "daughter colonies," see Kathleen Neils Conzen, "Making Their Own America: Assimilation Theory and the German Peasant Pioneer," German Historical Institute, Annual Lecture Series, no. 3 (Washington, D.C., 1990); Wilfred P. Schoenberg, S.J., *A History of the Catholic Church in the Pacific Northwest, 1743-1983* (Washington, D.C., 1987); Alan R. Anderson, "German Settlements in Saskatchewan," in Martin L. Kovacs, ed., *Roots and Realities Among Eastern and Central Europeans* (Edmonton, 1983), 175-221; *History of the Elkhorn Valley, Nebraska: An Album of History and Biography* (Chicago, 1892); and *Muenster, Texas: A Centennial History, 1889-1989* (Muenster, Texas, 1989).

10. Harry H. Anderson, ed., *German-American Pioneers in Wisconsin and Michigan: The Frank-Kerler Letters* (Milwaukee, 1971), 76.

11. For example, Charles J. Wallman, *The German Speaking 48ers: Builders of Watertown, Wisconsin* (Madison, 1990).

12. Heinrich Lemcke, *Wisconsin: Nach eigenen Erfahrungen und*

Beobachtungen. Übers Meer, vol. 3 (Leipzig, 1883), 123.

13. Carl F. Wehrwein, "Bonds of Maintenance as Aids in Acquiring Farm Ownership," in the *Journal of Land and Public Utility Economics*, 8 (1932), 396-403; Kathleen Neils Conzen, "Peasant Pioneers: Generational Succession Among German Immigrants in Frontier Minnesota," in Steven Hahn and Jonathan Prude, eds., *The Countryside in the Age of Capitalist Transformation: Essays in the Social History of Rural America* (Chapel Hill, 1985), 259-292; Gloria Wolpert, "The More Things Change: A Study of Intergenerational Land Transfer in Four Rural Wisconsin Communities" (doctoral dissertation, University of Chicago, 1994).

14. Calculated from *Outline Map of Dodge Co., Wisconsin* (Clinton, Iowa, 1910).

15. Wolpert, "The More Things Change"; O. F. Hoffman, "Culture of the Centreville-Mosel Germans in Manitowoc and Sheboygan Counties" (doctoral dissertation, University of North Carolina, 1942).

16. This scholarship is summarized in Kathleen Neils Conzen, "Die deutsche Amerikaeinwanderung im ländlichen Kontext: Problemfelder und Forschungsergebnisse," in Klaus J. Bade, ed., *Auswanderer—Wanderarbeiter—Gastarbeiter: Bevölkerung, Arbeitsmarkt und Wanderung in Deutschland seit der Mitte des 19. Jahrhunderts* (Ostfildern, Germany, 1984), 1:350-377.

17. For two recent efforts to explore the continuing salience of ethnic background for midwestern farming, see Mark W. Friedberger, *Farm Families and Change in Twentieth-Century America* (Lexington, 1988); and Sonya Salamon, *Prairie Patrimony: Family, Farming, and Community in the Midwest* (Chapel Hill, 1992).

Old Times, New Ways

1. Joseph Shafer's Wisconsin "Domesday Book" series, including *A History of Agriculture in Wisconsin* (Madison, 1922) and *The Winnebago-Horicon Basin: A Type Study in Western History* (Madison, 1937), describes the physical geography of Wisconsin in relation to settlement and agricultural development. See Merle Curti, *The Making of an American Community: A Case Study of Democracy in a Frontier Community* (Stanford, 1959). Jane Marie Pederson contrasts the high level of mobility during the early frontier years with the population stability of dairy farming in the later 1800s in a model study, *Between Memory and Reality: Family and Community in Rural Wisconsin, 1870-1970* (Madison, 1992).

2. See Lutz K. Berkner, "The Stem Family and the Developmental Cycle of the Peasant Household: An Eighteenth Century Austrian Example," in the *American Historical Review*, 77:2 (April, 1972); Jack Goody, Joan Thirsk, and E. P. Thompson, eds., *Family*

and *Inheritance: Rural Society in Western Europe, 1200-1800* (Cambridge, 1976); and David Gaunt, "Rural Household Organization and Inheritance in Northern Europe," in the *Journal of Family History*, 12: 121-142 (1987). For the midwestern context, see Mark W. Friedberger, "Handing Down the Home Place: Farm Inheritance Strategies in Iowa, 1870-1945," in *The Annals of Iowa*, 8:518-536 (1981). Marveen Minish, Lorena Evans' granddaughter, generously shared her unpublished research paper, "The American Agrarian Tradition in the Family of Marveen Minish" (1983).

3. Sheehan also describes rural female domestic service in *German History*. Rural sociologists and historians have examined work and decision-making on family farms, including several brief studies published by the University of Wisconsin-Madison, Agricultural Research Station [ARS]. See, for example, Eugene A. Wilkening, "Adoption of Improved Farm Practices as Related to Family Factors," ARS Bulletin no. 171 (Madison, 1953); Sloan R. Wayland, "Social Patterns of Farming," Columbia University Seminar on Rural Life (New York, 1951); Kenneth H. Parson and Erven J. Long, "How Family Labor Affects Wisconsin Farming," ARS Bulletin no. 167 (Madison, 1970); Gould P. Colman, "How Farm Families Make Decisions," Rural Sociology Bulletin Series (Ithaca, 1975-1976); Joan Vanek, "Work, Leisure, and Family Roles: Farm Households in the United States, 1920-1955," in *Journal of Family History*, 5:4 (Winter, 1980); and Eugene A. Wilkening, *Farm Husbands and Wives in Wisconsin: Work Roles, Decision Making and Satisfaction* (Madison, 1981). For women's work and the farm economy, see John Mack Faragher, "History from the Inside-Out: Writing the History of Women in Rural America," in *The American Quarterly*, 33:537-557 (1981); Mary Neth, *Preserving the Family Farm: Women, Community and the Foundation of Agribusiness in the Midwest, 1900-1940* (Baltimore, 1995); and Joan M. Jensen, *Promise to the Land: Essays on Rural Women* (Albuquerque, 1991).

4. Studies of regional agricultural history include Eric Lampard, *The Rise of the Dairy Industry in Wisconsin: A Study in Agricultural Change, 1860-1920* (Madison, 1963); Michael P. Conzen, *Frontier Farming in an Urban Shadow: The Influence of Madion's Proximity on the Agricultural Development of Blooming Grove, Wisconsin* (Madison, 1971); Allan G. Bogue, *From Prairie to Cornbelt: Farming on the Illinois and Iowa Prairies in the Nineteenth Century* (Chicago, 1963); John G. Thompson, *The Rise and Decline of the Wheat Growing Industry in Wisconsin*, Bulletin of the University of Wisconsin, Economics and Political Science Series, 5:3 (Madison, 1909); Terry G. Jordan and Matti Kaups, *The American Backwoods Frontier: An Ethnic and Ecological Interpretation* (Baltimore, 1989);

Terry G. Jordan, *German Seed in Texas Soil: Immigrant Farmers in Nineteenth-Century Texas* (Austin, 1966); and Robert P. Swierenga, "Ethnicity and American Agriculture," in *Ohio History*, 89:323-344 (1980). Robert Banning, *All Is Not Butter* (Boston, 1954) describes everyday life among Wisconsin's German farmers. The following unpublished research reports for Old World Wisconsin, State Historical Society of Wisconsin, provided background on Pomeranian immigrant farming: Olivia Mahoney, "Daily Life of the Pomeranians: A Report for Interpretation" (1979); Marty Perkins, "The Friedrich Koepsell Farm: A Pomeranian Carpenter's Farmstead of Washington County, c. 1880" (1976); and Mark Knipping, "The Charles Schulz Farm: A Pomeranian Wheat Farm of Dodge County, Wisconsin, c. 1860" (1976).

5. See Timothy L. Smith, "Religion and Ethnicity in America," in the *American Historical Review*, 83:1155-1185 (December, 1978). The following manuscripts, minutes, and histories of local churches illuminated the tensions and sources of schisms within churches: *By the Grace of God: Trinity Evangelical Lutheran Church of Freistadt* (1964), and Adolph G. Pankow, "Complete Genealogy of Descendants of the Rev. Erdman Pankow," unpublished manuscript in the research files of Old World Wisconsin (Eagle, Wisconsin); and *First Congregational Church History, 1976*, pamphlet, Watertown Historical Society. Allan Krause kindly provided access to an unpublished translation of the Lebanon Baptist Church Register. Reports from the regional Baptist Convention suggested the ambiguous position of German-language parishes; see Edgar L. Killam, *Centennial History of the Wisconsin Baptist Convention* (Milwaukee, 1944) and *Minutes of the Lake Shore Baptist Association* (Milwaukee, 1858, 1862, 1882, and 1883).

Iowa photograph by Rexford Krueger. WHi(X3)38066

Photography and Autobiography

1. Naomi Rosenblum, *A History of Women Photographers* (New York, 1994), takes the artistic intentions of amateur photographers seriously and explores the genres they have pursued.

2. George A. Talbot wrote the initial version of "Reading Pictures" for the State Historical Society of Wisconsin's exhibition "Six Generations Here: A Family Remembers" (1982). John Collier, Jr., *Visual Anthropology: Photography as a Research Method* (New York, 1967) is a valuable manual for the social historian. In addition, see "Photographs and the Study of the Past," James Borchert's appendix to *Alley Life in Washington: Family, Community, Religion, and Folklife in the City, 1850-1970* (Urbana, 1982), 269-303; Howard S. Becker, "Photography and Sociology," in *Studies in the Anthropology of Visual Communication,* 1:1, 3-26 (1974); Michael Bell and Steven Ohrn, eds., "Saying Cheese: Studies in Folklore and Visual Communication," an issue of *Folklore Forum,* Special and Bibliographic Series, no. 13 (Bloomington, 1975); Judith Mara Gutman, "Family Photo Interpretation," in *Kin and Communities,* ed. by Allan J. Lichtman and Joan Challinor (Washington, 1979); Graham King, *Say 'Cheese'! Looking at Snapshots in a New Way* (New York, 1984); and Alan Trachtenberg, *Reading American Photographs: Images as History—Mathew Brady to Walker Evans* (New York, 1989). See also Michael Lesy, *Wisconsin Death Trip* (New York, 1973); John Berger, "The Suit and the Photograph," in *About Looking* (New York, 1980); and Lizabeth A. Cohen, "Embellishing a Life of Labor: An Interpretation of the Material Culture of American Working-Class Homes, 1885-1915," in the *Journal of American Culture,* 3:752-775 (Winter, 1980).

3. See John Modell, "Patterns of Consumption, Acculturation, and Family Income Strategies in Late Nineteenth-Century America," in *Family and Population in Nineteenth-Century America,* ed. by Tamara Hareven and Maris Vinovskis (Princeton, 1978), and Kerreen M. Reiger, *The Disenchantment of the Home: Modernizing the Australian Family, 1880-1940* (New York, 1985).

4. For reading meaning in images, see Julia Hirsch, *Family Photographs: Content, Meaning and Effect* (New York, 1981) and Alan Thomas, *Time in a Frame: Photography and the Nineteenth-Century Mind* (New York, 1977). In a brief, compelling essay, "The Democratization of the Portrait," Alain Corbin discusses photography in the "development of individual self awareness," *From the Fires of Revolution to the Great War,* ed. by Michele Perrot, volume 4 in the five-volume *History of Private Life* (Cambridge, 1990). Mark Silber discovered a cache of negatives by Gilbert Wight Tilton and Fred W. Record stored in a Maine barn, from which he compiled *The Family Album: Photographs of the 1890s and 1900s* (Boston, 1973).

Expanding Horizons

1. Popular and scholarly publications on local history include Elmer Kiesling, *Watertown Remembered* (Watertown, Wisconsin, 1976); anon., *The History of Dodge County* (Chicago, 1880); Homer Bishop Hubbel, *Dodge County, Wisconsin: Past and Present* (Chicago, 1913); Watertown Wisconsin Centennial, *The Past Our Heritage, the Future Our Challenge, 1854-1954* (Watertown, Wisconsin, 1954); William F. Whyte, "Settlement of Lebanon, Dodge County," in the *Proceedings* of the State Historical Society of Wisconsin, (1915) 99-110; and Joseph Schafer, "The Yankee and the Teuton in Wisconsin," in the *Wisconsin Magazine of History,* 6:125-145 (1922-1923).

2. Alexander Krueger is listed as a first-year student in the agricultural short course in the *Badger Yearbook* for 1897-1898. See also Merle Curti and Vernon Carstensen, *The University of Wisconsin: A History, 1848-1925* (2 vols., Madison, 1949).

3. Kirk Jeffrey, "The Family as Utopian Retreat from the City," in *Soundings,* 55:1 (Spring, 1972).

Immigrant Stories

1. Paul Thompson *et al.* have advanced the interdisciplinary study of family stories in *Between Generations: Family Models, Myths and Memories* (Oxford, 1993). Studies of personal and family narratives include: Sandra Dolby Stahl, *Literary Folkloristics and the Personal Narrative* (Bloomington, 1988); L. Langness and Gelya Frank, *Lives: An Anthropological Approach to Biography* (Novato, California, 1981); Jan Vansina, *Oral Tradition: A Study in Historical Methodology* (Chicago, 1965); and Steven J. Zeitlin, *et al., A Celebration of American Family Folklore: Tales and Traditions from*

Iowa pigs photographed by Rexford Krueger. WHi Lot 3994/133

the *Smithsonian Collection* (New York, 1982). Monographs on family and life stories include Juha Pentikainen's *Oral Repertoire and World View: An Anthropological Study of Marina Takalo's Life History* (Helsinki, Finland, 1978); Kathryn L. Morgan's *Children of Strangers: The Stories of a Black Family* (Philadelphia, 1980); Leonard W. Roberts' *Up Kutshin and Down Greasy: Folkways of a Kentucky Mountain Family* (Lexington, 1959); and Karen L. Baldwin's doctoral dissertation, "Down on Bugger Run: Family Group and the Social Base of Folklore" (University of Pennsylvania, 1975). In addition, see Margaret R.Yocom's dissertation,"Fieldwork in Family Folklore and Oral History: A Study in Methodology" (University of Massachusetts, Amherst, 1980); and Barbara Allen, "Family Tradition and Personal Identity," in the *Kentucky Folklore Record*, 28 (1982).

2. Lynwood Montell, *Saga of Coe Ridge* (New York, 1972); and Sandra Dolby Stahl, "Family Settlement Stories and Personal Values," in *The Old Traditional Way of Life: Essays in Honor of Warren E. Roberts*, ed. by Robert E. Walls and George H. Schoemaker (Bloomington, 1989), 362-366. Robert E. McGlone examines the dynamics of family narrative revision in "Rescripting a Troubled Past: John Brown's Family and the Harpers Ferry Conspiracy," in the *Journal of American History*, 75:1179-1200 (March,1989).

3. See Robert Harms, "Oral Tradition and Ethnicity," in the *Journal of Interdisciplinary Studies*, 10:1 (1979). On immigration and assimilation, see also: Milton Gordon, *Assimilation in American Life: The Role of Race, Religion, and National Origins* (New York, 1964); Virginia Yans McLaughlin, ed., *Immigration Reconsidered: History, Sociology and Politics* (New York, 1990); Walter Kamphoefner, "Interdisciplinary Perspectives on Rural Immigration and Ethnicity," in the *Journal of American Ethnic History*, 14:47-52 (Summer, 1995); and a review of the scholarship in Russel A. Kazal, "Revising Assimilation: The Rise, Fall, and Reappraisal of a Concept of American Ethnic History," in the *American Historical Review*, 100:437-471 (April, 1995).

4. Larger issues of memory and national identity are examined in David Thelen's "Memory and American History," in the *Journal of American History*, 75:1117-1129 (March, 1989), and in John Bodnar's *Remaking America: Public Memory, Commemoration, and Patriotism in the Twentieth Century* (Princeton, 1992).

Landscapes of Farm Family Life

1. Quoted from *Land of the Free* (New York, 1938). See John Fraser Hart, *The Look of the Land* (Englewood Cliffs, New Jersey, 1975); J. Ritchie Garrison's *Landscape and Material Life in Franklin County, Massachusetts, 1770-1860* (Knoxville, 1991); and Robert P. Swierenga, "Theoretical Perspectives on the New Rural History: From Environmentalism to Modernism," in *Agricultural History*, 56:495-502 (Fall, 1982). See also Cary Carson, "Doing History with Material Culture," in *Material Culture and the Study of American Life*, ed. by Ian M. G. Quimby (New York, 1978), 41-64; Dell Upton, "The Power of Things: Recent Studies in American Vernacular Architecture," in *The American Quarterly*, 35:279-295 (Spring, 1983); and Thomas Schlereth, ed., *Material Culture Studies in America* (Nashville, 1982).

2. See Sally McMurry, *Families and Farmhouses in Nineteenth-Century America: Vernacular Design and Social Change* (New York, 1988), and Fred W. Peterson, "Vernacular Building and Victorian Architecture: Midwestern American Farm Homes," in the *Journal of Interdisciplinary History*, 12:409-428 (Winter, 1982).

3. Bruce Levine, *The Spirit of 1848: German Immigrants, Labor Conflict, and the Coming of the Civil War* (Urbana, 1992), traces German ethnic political activism. See also Roger E. Wyman, "Wisconsin Ethnic Groups and the Election of 1890," in the *Wisconsin Magazine of History*, 51:269-293 (Summer, 1968); Dan Harrison Doyle, *The Social Order of a Frontier Community: Jacksonville, Illinois, 1825-1870* (Urbana, 1978); and E. L. Luther, "Farmers' Institutes in Wisconsin, 1885-1993," in the *Wisconsin Magazine of History*, 30:59-68 (September, 1946).

4. See Grant McCracken, *Culture and Consumption: New Approaches to the Symbolic Character of Consumer Goods and Activities* (Bloomington, 1990). On changing material expectations, see Clifford E. Clark, Jr., *The American Family Home, 1800-1960* (Chapel Hill, 1986); Sally McMurry, "City Parlor, Country Sitting Room: Rural Vernacular Design and the American Parlor, 1840-1900," in the *Winterthur Portfolio*, 20:261-280 (Winter, 1985); Dolores Hayden, *Redesigning the American Dream: The Future of Housing, Work, and Family Life* (New York, 1984); and Elaine Tyler May, *Great Expectations: Marriage and Divorce in Post-Victorian America* (Chicago, 1980). See also William Seale's *The Tasteful Interlude: American Interiors Through the Camera's Eye* (Nashville, 1981).

5. Consult Warren E. Roberts, *Viewpoints on Folklife: Looking at the Overlooked* (Ann Arbor, 1988), as well as Jeanette Lasasky, *Willow, Oak, and Rye* (Philadelphia, 1979); Ernst Schlee, *German Folk Art* (New York, 1980); and Karl E. Wald Fritzch and Manfred Bachmann, *An Illustrated History of German Toys* (New York, 1978).

6. On reading artifacts and domestic interiors, see Simon J. Bronner, *Folklife Studies from the Gilded Age: Object, Rite, and Custom in Victorian America* (Ann Arbor, 1989), and Maxine Van de Wettering, "The Nineteenth Century Concept of Home," in the *Journal of American Studies*, 18:5-28 (April, 1984).

7. Yi-Fu Tuan, *Space and Place: The Perspective of Experience* (Minneapolis, 1977), and *Segmented Worlds and Self: Group Life and Individual Consciousness* (Minneapolis, 1982).

THE KRUEGER GENERATIONS HERE

First Generation
Wilhelm Krüger—Anglicized to **William Krueger (1818-1908)**—and his wife **Wilhelmina** (Minnie) and three children emigrated in 1851 from Pomerania, a province of east Prussia bordering the Baltic Sea, leaving behind his parents Martin and Sophia Krüger, and brother Heinrich. Once in America they settled in the rural township of Emmet in Dodge County, in southeastern Wisconsin. After Minnie died, William remarried twice, his third wife being **Johanna Siden**.

Second Generation
When Minnie died in 1870, William was left with six children ranging in age from eight to twenty-five. The oldest son, **August (1845-1923)**, married **Mary Goetsch**, literally "the girl next door," in 1871. Other second generation Kruegers married into the extended William and Charlotte Goetsch family: sister Bertha married Mary's brother **William E. Goetsch**, (sometimes referred to in the text as "Aunt Bertha" and "Uncle Bill") and Emilie married a Goetsch cousin, Charles Goetsch. August and Mary provided a home for his youngest brothers, **Albert** and **Henry** (born in 1861) until they left the farm in adulthood. Mary's sister **Martha Sara Goetsch** married August Buelke, and their boys were Willie and Ernie.

Third Generation
August Krueger was twenty-seven and his wife Mary twenty, when their first child, **Alexander (Alex)** was born in 1872. A daughter, **Saraphine (Sarah)** was born in 1875. **Alex (1872-1948)** in turn married the "girl next door," **Florentina (Flora) Will**. Their twins were born in 1899 and that's when much of the picture-taking begins. Sarah married in 1914 and moved off the family farm to nearby Watertown.

Other family picture-takers of this generation were two cousins: **Rexford Krueger,** who married Winifred (Winnie) Evans in 1918, and **Willie Buelke**.

A number of elderly relatives of this generation and the next were interviewed for the "Six Generations Here" project, including Albert Krueger's daughter **Selma Krueger Abel**, August and Mary Krueger's nephew **Anson Goetsch** and his Iowa cousin **Lorena Goetsch Evans**.

Fourth Generation
Alex and Flora's twins **Edgar and Jennie** were photographed repeatedly throughout childhood. When Edgar married Elna Sommerfield in 1929, they joined the older generations on the farm and the picture-taking continued with grandfather Alex photographing Edgar and Elna's children Shirley and Robert. Edgar's twin sister married Ernst Breutzman in 1920.

Edgar Krueger (1899-1988) was 76 when this project began, and, as the recognized family chronicler, was a major source of family stories. Edgar's second cousin, **Lester Buelke,** maintained his father Willie Buelke's collection of family artifacts, together with his glass-plate negatives.

Fifth Generation
When **Shirley** grew up she married Delbert Oestreich, and in 1960 her brother **Robert (Bob) Krueger** married Delbert's cousin Beatrice (Bea) Oestreich.

Sixth Generation
This Krueger generation consists of Shirley and Delbert Oestreich's three sons: **Glenn, Paul,** and **Dale**.

At the opening of the exhibit "Six Generations Here: A Family Remembers" at Old World Wisconsin in 1982, the modern Krueger clan posed in front of an enlargement of the family portrait from 1900. The Kruegers and their relatives interviewed for this project include Edgar Krueger (1899–1988), seated between his two children, Shirley and Bob; as well as Bob's wife Bea; Shirley's husband Delbert; and their sons, Dale, Paul, and Glenn. Photograph by Dennis Church. WHi 98975